Contents

The World of Robert Burns by
   Tamas McDonald   5

The Poetry of Robert Burns by
   David Daiches   36

A Selection of Burns's Poetry   43

Animal Poems
   The Death and Dying Words of Poor Mailie—43:
   Poor Mailie's Elegy—44: To a Mouse—45: The Auld
   Farmer's New-Year Morning's Salutation to His Auld Mare,
   Maggie—47

Satires
   Address to the Unco Guid—50: Holy Willie's Prayer—52:
   The Twa Dogs—54

Letters and Addresses
   Epistle to Davie—60: Second Epistle to J. Lapraik—62:
   Epistle to a Young Friend—65: To William Creech—67:
   To a Louse—68: To a Haggis—70: Address to the Deil—71

Descriptive and Narrative Poems
   The Cotter's Saturday Night—74: Tam o' Shanter—79:

Songs
   Mary Morison—84: There was a Lad—85: Up in the
   Morning Early—86: I Love my Jean—86: My Bonie
   Mary—86: Afton Water—87: Ay Waukin, O—88:
   John Anderson, My Jo—88: The Banks O' Doon—89:
   Hey, Ca' Thro'—89: The Deil's Awa wi' th' Exciseman—90:
   The Lea Rig—90: Duncan Gray—91: Robert Bruce's March
   to Bannockburn—92: O, Whistle an' I'll Come to Ye, My
   Lad—93: A Red, Red Rose—93: Ca' the Yowes to the
   Knowes—94: For a' That and a' That—95: O, Wert Thou in
   the Cauld Blast—96: Auld Lang Syne—96

The World of Robert Burns

Few men of any country have achieved the worldwide reputation and inspired such international affection as has Robert Burns, Scotland's greatest poet. Burns Societies around the globe celebrate his birthday every year, while millions of people have read his verses and enjoyed his songs. The recognition that has come to him in the years since his early death was not so quick in coming during his life, however; many of his followers today would be surprised to learn that his life was a very hard one.

Burns was born in 1759, at a time when all of Britain was beginning to undergo great changes in the way people were earning their living and leading their lives. In Scotland, in the latter part of the eighteenth century, an explosion of cultural activity took place with Edinburgh as its focus. All Europe marvelled at Scottish achievements in architecture, science, painting, medicine and writing; and in poetry the speakers of Scots found a new articulate champion in an Ayrshire farmer, Robert Burns.

Burns was born in the village of Alloway in the south-western Lowlands of Scotland. The chief means of support in this part of the country was the land, and an era of peace following the Union of England and Scotland in 1707 and the final defeat of the Jacobite claim to the throne in 1745 encouraged a new interest in farming. The land was experiencing an 'agrarian revolution', and times were hard.

Life in the Lowlands

Landowners

Some people owned the land, and many people worked it; they were seldom the same people. Those who owned the land and collected the rents generally lived very comfortably; the wealthier among them would often maintain a house in Edinburgh as well as their country house. They enjoyed political power through representation at Westminster, and held rights in their own parish to assist in the examination

A drawing of the cottage at Alloway in Ayrshire where Burns was born.

of the schoolmaster and to nominate the local minister. Their status in relation to their own tenants was very much like that of father to son, but the system was economically heavily weighted against the farmer nevertheless. Whether he was a 'gudeman' or tenant farmer, a 'cottar' or a farm labourer, he would find it necessary to work long hours in any weather so as to make ends meet.

The Old System

Before the sweeping changes that took place during the years of Burns' childhood, most of the farming in the Lowlands was done by the 'infield-outfield run-rig' system. Farms were seldom individual holdings but were run co-operatively by groups of peasants who would divide the infield land into long strips or rigs. The total area would be as much as they could keep under cultivation at any time with the number of ploughing teams they had at their disposal. This farming unit was known as a 'farmtoun' or, if it happened to contain the church of the parish, a 'kirktoun' or 'clachan'.

Rent to the landlord was almost always in kind rather than in cash: thus, for every seed that went into the ground, one from the yield went to replace it and another paid the rent. What was left was the

6

farmer's net yield—one seed for every one sown. Obviously, farm workers did not get rich and their diet was, of necessity, very basic.

Food

With oats as the most common crop, porridge formed the staple part of many meals, and could be supplemented by oat cakes or bannocks—buns or small loaves made from unleavened oat or barley flour. The barley itself was of a rough variety known as 'bear' and was most commonly used in the brewing of ale. Barley bannocks made a good snack because they could be chewed all day. Oat bannocks were more tasty and went down more easily, especially when they were smeared with thickened oxen blood, drawn from the living animal and boiled into a thick paste.

Variety was achieved through the introduction of basic greens into the diet, and any vegetable broth cooked up in the kailpot could be thickened with the addition of oatmeal. Meat would be added from time to time by the farm animals, particularly at the beginning of winter, when all the animals not required for breeding would be slaughtered and the meat pickled in brine. The real treat was haggis, cooked from those parts of the animal which would otherwise rot very quickly. The rest of the carcase might be sold off but the liver, heart, kidneys and intestines would be chopped up, mixed with oatmeal and ox blood, and then boiled for several hours in a sheep's stomach.

Housing

The animals maintained on the early Lowland farms were not well-kept and could not have led very contented lives. They grazed on the outfield or common pasture land and, in bitter weather, would be brought into the house. Until conditions changed for the better in the latter half of the century, the stench in the farmers' houses was always appalling. Burns was to say of his father's house that he could sit by the fire and be struck by the sight and the smell of waste, both animal and human, and by the sound of the rats scurrying about in the darkness.

Tenant farmers had better houses than farm workers, where workers had houses at all. Often, the

'An evening in a Scots Cottage' painted by Alexander Carse. For an idea of what sort of social life might be enjoyed in such a barren little hovel look at one of Burns' own poems: 'The Cotter's Saturday Night' is a touching and instructive portrait of a poor family enjoying their repose at the end of a busy week. The quality of their hospitality and the devotion of their religion are two of the most striking characteristics of the cottar's life.

poor cottar would find his shelter in one of the two rooms in the 'gudeman's' house, the room that was known as the 'but'. As this was also the kitchen, it was the social focus of the farm. The other room was called the 'ben', and was the room shared by the farmer, his wife, their children and the family cow.

The cottars' houses were much simpler and more primitive; often constructed of mud, turf and wooden stakes, they were held together by a clumsy mortar comprised of straw and clay. The better houses were constructed of stone with walls all of five feet high and twelve feet long, but here again the earth itself would provide the floor and the furnishings were sparse. The essential item of furniture was always the box bed, enclosed on all sides and accessible by a sliding door in the front. A house within a house, it offered a precious extra measure of protection against the elements, all the more important in the houses which did not have chimneys but simply let the smoke from the hearth escape through a hole in the roof.

The Church in the middle of the eighteenth century was not as strict and powerful as it had been one hundred years earlier, but it was still a strong force in the community. The 'presbyteries' or councils of ministers and elders elected by the congregation of each parish, maintained a fairly close watch on the life of every community, careful that nobody in the parish failed to keep the Sabbath holy, and ensuring that every member of the community led a Christian life. Offenders were brought before the 'Kirk session' and made to repent in public for their wrongdoing, while the minister lectured the congregation on the evils of sin.

It was laid down by statute that every Lowland country parish was to have its own school and by 1760 this had been achieved. This by no means solved the problems of education, though; parishes could be huge and attendances could be irregular if the child had far to go, or was required at home to help with the harvest. An alternative was provided by the 'adventure schools', organised independently of the parish authorities and existing on the modest

Religion and Education

'A Schule Skailin' by George Harvey shows a school typical of the kind that Burns attended. His schoolmaster, John Murdoch was to be a great influence on Burns' life, and in later years brought many men of wit and intellect to his farm for evenings of conversation and debate.

fees charged to the parents for the hiring of the school and schoolmaster. It was just such a school that Robert Burns attended.

Writing and arithmetic were taught in all the schools although the adventure schools provided little opportunity for a grounding in the classics or religious studies. Discipline was hard and conditions harsh. Pupils would write sprawled out on the muddy floor where there was no furniture, and the draughty schoolhouses provided little shelter against the damp and the cold. Candles were often beyond the school's budget and books other than the Bible were not common.

Despite all that was lacking in the educational system, it made for an almost totally literate population. Numerous accounts exist of the number of books even in cottars' houses; the country was well-prepared to receive the great cultural advances of the last half of the century.

The Decline of Superstition

Another gradual effect of the spread of education was the development of a new sophistication and a decline of superstition among the people. An end to the hideous persecution of witches was reached at last in 1727 when a poor old woman was strangled for supposedly having turned her daughter into a pony. In 1736 the laws against witchcraft were repealed, and so began the march away from the gentle superstition of medieval times and the fiercer persecution of witches by the early Presbyterian Church.

Ancient beliefs remained a part of Scottish folklore, but they represented less of a threat in this more educated age. Robert Burns told of an old widow and her vast collection of tales and songs involving witches, devils, ghosts, fairies, giants and enchanted towers, but these did not terrify so much as fire the imagination of the poet and storyteller. His poems, 'Tam o' Shanter' and 'Hallowe'en' capture the spirit in which these creatures of darkness were appreciated.

Medicine

Superstition took a little longer to die in the practice of medicine. The great advances that were to give

Scotland's medical schools such a high international reputation were still a good fifty years away, and in the Lowlands of Scotland in the mid-eighteenth century it was not uncommon for an illness to be treated by waving a Bible over a sick person. That 'cure' might not have been harmful, however ineffectual it was, but often the cures were as dangerous as the disease. Not surprising, perhaps, when drugs recommended to doctors in a medical textbook published in Edinburgh in 1737 included crushed toad, urine, ants' eggs, excrement of pig and peacock, woodlice juice and similar 'cures'. There were still many deadly diseases rife in the community—cholera, typhoid, rheumatic fever—the last of which was to kill Burns himself. Most deadly of all was smallpox; an epidemic could kill one in four of the population. A common complaint was skin rash—not surprising perhaps as it was often the habit amongst farm workers to have themselves sewn into their shirts in autumn and then break open their stitches in spring.

The doctors of the time were still largely ineffective, and we can laugh with Burns at the quack doctor in his poem, 'Death and Doctor Hornbrook', a

'Fruitseller' by Walter Geikie shows how the children of Burns' time dressed. The portrayal may be rather romanticised.

poor figure who is reported by the spectre of death as being responsible for more deaths than the spectre itself.

Social Life

'Pitlessie Fair' was painted by Sir David Wilkie a few years after Burns' death, but the country fairs of his day would have been very much like this. His poem 'The Holy Fair' was based on just such an event.

Despite the harshness of life, the disease and poverty, the stern eyes of the kirk ministers and their distaste for merry joviality, the Lowland peasantry still managed on occasion to have a good time. Children were put to work early, but while still young they would enjoy their games of tops, quoits and kites, their balls and ropes. Shinty teams were formed and curling became a popular winter pastime. For adults, country fairs and social weddings gave the entire community an opportunity to get together for merry-making. In Burns' poem 'The Holy Fair', we read of those occasional and special gatherings when thousands of people would come together from the parishes round about for a great sermon, followed by much laughter and dancing and the consumption of large quantities of 'nappy' or ale. Burns himself was to develop quite a weakness for it.

It was the success or failure of the gruelling work in the fields that determined the quality of life of the farmer.

By a process called 'enclosure', single compact farms run by a single tenant began to replace the old run-rig system, making farms more profitable but also casting many workers off the land. For those with money to spend on improvements, trees could be planted to protect the fields from wind erosion; barns built to house grain; marshland converted to good farmland using new techniques and newly-invented seed drills and threshing machines bought to improve efficiency at seeding and harvest time. The iron-swing plough, another invention, could be operated by fewer men than the old wooden one.

Oats and barley improved in quality, so animal herds became healthier. Meat was of a better quality and the milk yield increased. New fertilisers were developed, and different crops sown annually, leaving the field empty every four of five years so as not to exhaust the soil. New crops were introduced too—clover, turnips, rye-grass, and the potato. As a result, the diet became more varied, and the population healthier.

The New Developments

This, then was the world that Robert Burns was born into. His father, William Burnes (he spelled his name with an e) was a gardener by profession and had taken a number of jobs since leaving the farmland of his childhood in Kincardineshire, far to the north of Edinburgh. One of these jobs had involved helping to lay out 'The Meadows' in Scotland's capital.

Burnes moved to Ayrshire, in the south-western Lowlands, and married Agnes Broun who, like him, came from a strict Presbyterian family. In the village of Alloway, near Ayr, he built himself a clay cottage, which still stands, and rented seven acres of land for a vegetable garden. Into this cottage Robert was born. For the first six years of Robert's life, his father held the position of head gardener on the estate of a wealthy retired doctor. He gave this up in 1765, having decided to take a chance on renting a large farm of his own. His courage can be applauded more than his choice of farm, for Mount Oliphant, a few

Burns' Early Life

miles to the east, was seventy acres of badly-drained and tired soil, and the rent was steep. For twelve years, he and his growing family struggled hard to make this farm pay before William decided to give it up.

When his eldest son was moving into manhood, father and family moved ten miles to the north-east, to the one hundred and thirty acre farm of Lochlie. The rent was three times as high as it had been at Mount Oliphant and, despite the improvements in farming techniques and the eagerness to learn and work hard, William had to admit that he was fighting a losing battle. Seven years after moving to Lochlie, he was to die while still struggling to pay off his creditors.

A painting of Lochlie Farm by an anonymous artist.

Education

When Robert was six, his father and four other farming families grouped together to hire a young schoolmaster named John Murdoch to give their children a solid grounding in reading and writing. The literature with which the boy became thoroughly acquainted was English; Scottish folklore and traditions were picked up around the family hearth. At home, wide reading was encouraged and, in what free time the labours of the farm allowed him, Robert devoured every book he could find. Ambitious for his sons, William encouraged them in adult conversation while they were still young and, committed to their education, sent Robert away from the farm for the summer of 1775, so that he might learn surveying in Kirkoswald. This, however, was to be the limit of his formal schooling. Like many other Scottish children of poor parents, he was to have no grammar school or university education.

On the Farm

For the farm work itself, Robert proved himself well-suited. He could handle the plough as well as anybody and was doing a man's work at the age of fifteen. As his six brothers and sisters followed him into the labours of the farm, so they took on their share of the effort in trying to make Mount Oliphant pay. But they were fighting a losing battle. For Robert's part, the hard work and insufficient nutrition while he was still young caused him dull headaches at night and the first signs of the heart disease which was to end his life while he was still at the peak of his creative powers.

The First Love Song

By the time he left the farm for the summer of surveying, he had already been inspired by his attraction to a local girl to write a love song; when he returned from Kirkoswald at the summer's end, he had learned as much about young love and life in the taverns as he had about surveying, and he was writing love songs regularly. His attractions to writing and to women did not impress his father, especially when Robert went against his wishes by attending a country dancing school for a short period of time in order to improve his manners.

The first few years at Lochlie were relatively hopeful and happy ones for the entire family. Robert continued to find time for his writing and falling in love but the demands placed upon him, as eldest child, remained severe. In the endless hunt for increased productivity, Robert and his brother rented three acres of land from their father so as to experiment in the cultivation of flax.

Since the beginning of the century, the linen industry had been growing beyond what had been simply a cottage industry: weaving done in the farmers' homes. Not until around the turn of the century would the huge cotton mills become a feature of Scottish life, but in Burns' early years the possibilities for cultivating flax as a cash crop were becoming more widely recognised; in the summer of 1781, Burns travelled to Irvine, on the west coast, to learn the method of dressing flax.

As a change from the hard toil of farm labour and an escape from one of his more unhappy love affairs, Irvine expanded the young poet's horizons. He plunged into the social life of the town and, through his friendship with an educated young sailor named Richard Brown, began taking himself seriously as a poet.

Unfortunately, 1782 dawned on an unhappy note and was to usher in four particularly hard years which Burns was to find so dispiriting that he very nearly emigrated to Jamaica. As a tragic result of New Year's Eve carousing, a fire destroyed the flax-dressing shop which Burns had opened with another man. Penniless, he returned to Lochlie, where his father, suffering from a serious illness, was fast approaching bankruptcy. Within scarcely more than two years, the farm had failed and William Burnes, was dead.

Deciding to try again elsewhere in an effort to revive the family fortunes, Robert and his brother moved a few miles away to a farm called Mossgiel and, while studying books on the new agricultural methods and applying themselves with the usual enthusiasm to their labours in the fields, they tried hard to make it pay. Once again, however, a Burns family venture proved to be a failure almost from the start; the soil was thick and weak and did not respond.

During his time at Mossgiel, Robert Burns continued both his love affairs and his writing, now concerned not only with love songs but with poems— poems that celebrated the beauty and power of nature and poems that recounted the customs and hardships of rural life. A form which had become a

The Interior of the Kitchen at Mossgiel Farm' by Sir William Allen.

particular feature of Scottish writing was that of the verse letter, and in this Burns was especially successful and productive.

He also began writing verse satires against the strictness and what he saw as the hypocrisy of the Presbyterian Church and its ministers. 'Holy Willie's Prayer', makes fun of just such a figure and 'The Holy Fair', besides being an effective portrait of country life at the huge gatherings mentioned earlier, is also a hearty ridiculing of religious superstition and hypocrisy.

In part, his feelings for the Church can be explained by the humiliation he was made to undergo because of his relationship with a local girl, Jean Armour. She became pregnant and had twins by him in 1786 and, although Burns was prepared for marriage, her parents were horrified at the prospect of their daughter marrying so poor a man. Whatever happy thoughts he felt at the prospect of becoming a

Jean Armour,
Burns' wife.
family man, Burns was hurt by their rejection of him and by the Church forcing him to publicly do penance for having committed a serious sin.

The
Kilmarnock
Edition
Under pressure from the Church, stung by rejection in love and distressed by the failure of yet another farm, Burns began speaking seriously of leaving the

country. In order to raise some money and to put off his creditors, he arranged with a Kilmarnock printer named John Wilson to bring out a small volume of his poems. Despite the troubles of the previous year, he had been extremely productive in his writing and had reason to suppose that with this new venture he might enjoy a modest success.

Published on 31 July, 1786, the *Poems, Chiefly in the Scottish Dialect* were a huge and almost immediate success. Not only through the towns and villages of the surrounding countryside was the new poet highly praised, but in Edinburgh as well. It was not only the critics who appreciated the poems, but people in all ranks of society; once again, Burns began to think that perhaps his future lay in Scotland after all.

For the present however, the immediate need was to answer Edinburgh's call and go to enjoy his success as a new, national poet. The years that lay ahead were to present new complications, challenges, and delights, for Edinburgh at the end of 1786 was like no other town Robert Burns had ever been in before.

Life in the City

Society in 1786 had been experiencing changes as great in industry as in agriculture and, in the cities of Scotland, this was reflected in the way people were living. Great technological advances had been made in the cotton and iron industries and James Watt's invention of the steam engine in 1765 had done perhaps more than any other single invention to speed up production in the factories and so increase the amount of wealth in society. Transportation had changed as well: in the last half of the century, three thousand miles of roads were built in Scotland and the travelling time from Glasgow to Edinburgh was cut from almost two days to six hours.

One statistic which illustrates not only the increased industrial strength of the country at this time but also the growing popular interest in reading

Industrial Advance

and writing is that, by the time Burns was writing his first poems, the country was producing more than four hundred tons of paper a year. Thirty years previously, the annual average had been about eighty tons.

Unfortunately, the fruits of the Industrial and Agrarian Revolutions were not being shared equally among the people. Men, women and children worked long, hard hours in the mines and mills, maiming themselves in operating machinery and developing serious lung diseases—and all for a paltry wage which scarcely provided a living. In the case of the mineworkers, in many places the entire families were actually considered to be the property of the mine owner, and it was a harsh necessity of life that six-year-old girls had to carry half-hundredweight loads of coal away from the coal-face if the family were to survive.

'A View of Edinburgh' by Patrick Nasmyth shows what the city of Edinburgh looked like around the time that Burns went there.

Where the poor gathered in the cities, filth and overcrowding were the automatic results. Edinburgh was never anything like the industrial centre which Glasgow was to become in the next century, and it can be admitted that sanitary and living conditions did improve throughout the 1700s. Nevertheless, more than fifty thousand people crowded into Edinburgh's Old Town in 1778 meant that widespread sickness and squalor were inevitable. Wynds and closes stank of human waste and it was considered an improvement over past centuries to have a closet built out over the wynds so that the walls would not be fouled by excrement. Happiest was the man who owned a hat shop and did not himself go walking!

Living Conditions

Despite the living conditions of the bulk of Edinburgh's population in 1787, the city was undergoing exciting changes and enjoying a growing international reputation for the excellence of its artists, scientists and teachers. In the twenty years previous to Burns' arrival in the city, much new building had been carried out in the New Town, under the direction of architects like Robert Adam, who found their inspiration in the classical models of ancient Greece and Rome. It was to these new, more spacious buildings and out of the cramped quarters of the Old Town that the leaders of Edinburgh society were moving: the lawyers, academics and the rural landowners with an interest in maintaining an elegant town house in more gracious surroundings than the Old Town could provide.

The Cultural Boom

The lawyers and landed gentry had very little direct interest in the arts and sciences themselves, in the sense that it was not these people who wrote the verses and made the new discoveries—there are of course, magnificient exceptions, notably Sir Walter Scott. Increased wealth in society had combined with improved standards of education to create new ideas as to how to live well, and this included the sponsorship of artists and craftsmen in the pursuit of a more comfortable life in more congenial surroundings. Large country and town houses had to

The Life of the Gentry

'*Bakehouse Close*' *by T A Newton. In another of Edinburgh's closes, Anchor Close, William Smellie, Burns' printer, had his workshop.*

be designed and built and then filled with the best new furniture, paintings, carpets and porcelain. Where something was not available locally, it had to be imported.

England was now quite unashamedly the model for the genteel classes and men and women took their lead in fashion from their counterparts on the other side of the border. Coats of finest English cloth and full dresses of velvet and silk sported broad cuffs and a great deal of jewellery. Ruffled shirts and tanned leather shoes were common and even children succumbed to the fashion: they might dress as coarsely as ever for everyday, but special occasions had them dressed fully like adults in miniature. The crowning touch, among adults, was the hair: men shaved both face and head and wore wigs, sometimes spending as much on two wigs as a farmworker earned in a year. With the ladies, long hair was drawn up over wire frames and was greased and powdered before being decorated with ribbons or feathers.

Food and drink were as obvious a part of life of the gentry as were the big houses, expensive furniture and fine clothes. Lavish meals could involve as many as fifty courses, and even a small meal such as breakfast could take two hours. As much drink as food was consumed, including such quantities of whisky, rum, wine and brandy that only rarely would a guest surprise the servants by making it to bed unaided.

Higher education also followed an English model. Youngsters of the gentry, after a childhood of private tuition with the family tutor, would enrol at a university such as Edinburgh or perhaps even Oxford or Cambridge. Holidays were spent on tours of the Continent and Ireland, so as to broaden the education.

The University

Edinburgh University was at this time at the height of its influence. Advances in philosophy, physics, chemistry and medicine had brought it to the attention of the world and its enrolment numbered more than a thousand. Even at the recently founded Royal High School, the enrolment was as high as five hundred. The educational system may not have been comprehensive—one third of the city's population remained illiterate throughout this period. It was, however, intense. Professors at Edinburgh had an extremely high reputation throughout Europe for the dynamic power of their lectures—spurred on, no doubt, because the salaries they collected depended very largely on the number of students they attracted.

The Arts

Finally, in painting and writing, the Scottish capital was experiencing a new prosperity. David Wilkie and the portrait painters Henry Raeburn and the younger Allan Ramsay established reputations which carried their names throughout Europe. Walter Scott was not to begin writing until after the turn of the century, but he was growing up in Edinburgh in this very fertile period, and was fascinated at his meeting with Burns. Poets like the older Allan Ramsay and Robert Fergusson, who died very young in 1774, had preceded Burns with their verses in the Scottish dialect. They had left the ground clear for Burns' startling arrival on the literary scene.

C M Hardie's painting of the meeting between Burns and the young Scott in Professor Fergusson's home, Sciennes House.

Burns' Tavern, Libberton Wynd by G Cattermole. A typical Edinburgh close of the mid-late eighteenth century.

Burns' Last Years

In all the higher circles of Edinburgh society, Robert Burns was given an enthusiastic reception. He was invited to dinners and parties and celebrated as the great farmer-poet. To a man less canny and sensitive than he was, all that instant fame might have appeared to guarantee his future in the capital.

Burns' reception in Edinburgh

Burns, however, was clever enough to see that much of the praise he was receiving was for the novelty value of his being a farmer who not only wrote good poetry but wrote it in Scots. In most cases, their admiration was genuine enough, but he knew that when the novelty wore off, he could be left stranded—the country genius cut off in the city.

One feature of Edinburgh life that greatly distressed him was the vast difference that existed between those with money and a 'good background' and those that had neither. He had attacked this difference years before when he had seen his father ground down by debt and poverty. In poems like 'The Twa Dogs', we are given a clear idea as to how Burns felt about the monied class. Once in Edinburgh, he was honest enough to recognise real worth where it did exist in some members of the gentry but, on the whole, their pomposity, hypocrisy and lavish habits made him very angry.

What was more, there were few among them who were his intellectual equal; various accounts survive of Burns' wit and clever mind. He was a powerful thinker and talker who could only have been annoyed at those members of the upper class who appreciated his poetic genius but still treated him like a farm boy.

A painting of Burns at Lord Monbaddo's house; Burns gave poetry readings at the houses of many noblemen during his sojourn in Edinburgh. At one of these houses he was introduced to William Creech, who brought out the second edition of his poetry.

He made many friends among this group but made others in the taverns and streets of the Old Town, where he would enjoy loud evenings of drinking and bawdy songs that would have shocked many genteel ears in the New Town.

Within a year of his arrival in the capital, he had met a literary agent named William Creech and agreed to publish a further edition of his poetry. Creech turned out to be one of the less happy of Burns' acquaintances: Burns sold him the copyright for one hundred guineas and made substantial money only on the subscription copies— the copies sold prior to publication. Creech had a habit of making Burns wait for his money and, on a

A portrait of William Creech by Sir Henry Raeburn. Creech was not the most prompt of men where it came to handing out payments, and Burns was moved to write irritably of him in his poem 'Willie's Awa': 'The stiffest o' them a' he bow'd, The bouldest o' them a' he cow'd.'

third, two-volume edition of his poems brought out in 1793, this man so arranged the poet's affairs that Burns received no payment at all apart from a few free copies of his own work. He was not destined to become rich on the earnings from his poetry.

The Edinburgh Edition For better or worse, the Edinburgh edition came out on 21 April, 1787, and made Robert Burns famous throughout the world. Included with the twenty-two new poems were five songs, a hint of his greatest work still to come.

Sir

Monday next is a day of the year with me hallowed as the ceremonies of Religion and sacred to the memory of the sufferings of my King and my Forefathers. — The honour you do me by your invitation I most cordially and gratefully accept. —

Tho' something like moisture conglobes in my eye,
Let no one misdeem me disloyal;
A poor friendless Wanderer may well claim a sigh,
Still more if that Wanderer were royal! —
My fathers that Name have rever'd on a throne;
My fathers have died to right it;
Those fathers would spurn their degenerate son,
That Name should he scoffingly slight it.

St James' sq.}
Weden: even.}
I am, Sir,
your obliged humble serv.t
Rob.t Burns

James Stewart Esq.r

Cleland's garden

Opposite *William Smellie printer of Burns' poems. Smellie took Burns under his wing, and through him Burns met many men of influence.*

Left *Facsimile of a letter from Burns to James Stewart Esq. accepting an invitation to be present at a Jacobite celebration— he was a staunch supporter of the Jacobite cause, as he was of the French Revolution.*

Below *A painting by C M Hardie of Burns reciting poems at the home of the Duchess of Gordon in 1787.*

A Silhouette of 'Clarinda', Mrs Agnes Maclehose. A correspondence between Burns and Mrs Maclehose started when on the day appointed for Burns' visit to her home, he injured his knee. Burns addressed her as 'Clarinda' and signed himself 'Sylvander'. His letters reveal a clear, intellectual witty and sensitive mind. Burns helped Mrs Maclehose to get her own poems published.

A New Ambition

But something else had originally brought Burns to Edinburgh. For worthy men of slender means, it often happened that a post was obtained for them in the Excise Service, whose function it was to regulate taxes on manufactured goods, control weights and measures through the country and prevent smuggling. To Burns, appointment to such a post would mean relief at last from the strains of farming and more opportunity to pursue his literary career. Unfortunately, many of the people who might have been able to help him secure such a post appeared to think that the rural genius and poet of the plough belonged back in his field and behind his plough. It was to be three long years before a minor position in the Excise Service was made available to him.

Back on the farm, his reputation as a poet and man

about town had changed the Armours' minds about his suitability as a husband for their daughter. Still hurt by their earlier rejection and now very much annoyed at their hypocrisy, he embarked on a tour of the Borders followed by two tours through the Highlands.

Tours of the Highlands were very popular but for Burns they were not simply undertaken for fun or to while away the time in remote parts while he waited for a vacancy to appear in the Excise Service. By this time, he had met in Edinburgh a man who had invented a cheap process for printing music and who had embarked upon a project of collecting together Scottish songs. The collection, entitled *The Scots Musical Museum*, was to involve many volumes and consume almost all of Burns poetic energies until 1792, when he would provide a similar service to another man assembling a volume entitled *Select Scottish Airs*. On both projects, he worked without payment, not so much unwisely as with unquestioning enthusiasm for two projects which captured his imagination and which he saw as of vital importance to preserving the folk traditions of Scotland.

The Highland Tours

Throughout his travels he listened for snippets of old melodies and verse and recorded any details of historical tradition of folk lore, also keeping a record of those spots of physical beauty which attracted his eye.

When he returned from his Highland tours, Burns was virtually editor of *The Scots Musical Museum*. In the years that remained to him, he was only to write one more narrative poem of any great importance. His critics agree that 'Tam o' Shanter', written in 1791 and published in Creech's two-volume edition of Burns' poetry in 1793, might very well have established his reputation as a poet even if it had been his only poem. True or not, Burns had other things on his mind when he returned from the Highlands: poetry took second place now while his work on Scotland's folk musical tradition was to occupy his time practically until the day he died.

Marriage   His proud refusal to become involved in discussing payment for his work on the songs and the dishonourable approach of his partners in these ventures in offering him nothing for his labour did not make the hardships of life any easier. One of his earlier problems was solved when he decided at last to marry Jean Armour and leave the farm at Mossgiel to his brother. In June of 1788, he took out a lease on the farm of Ellisland, near Dumfries, and was joined there six months later by Jean and his one surviving child.

Once again, however, despite his hard work, a farm was doomed to fail under his direction and, when a job in the Excise Service was offered to him in 1789, his days at Ellisland were numbered. For two more years he tried hard to make the farm pay but neither as an arable farm growing oats nor as a dairy farm did Ellisland show any promise. In November of 1791, he gave up the lease and moved into Dumfries, where he worked as an Excise Officer until his death.

Problems with Authority   Accounts of his life tell us that Burns made a good Exciseman, but this was not enough to keep him out of controversy. The uprising of the lower classes against the King and aristocracy in France in 1789 fired his democratic spirit and called into question his loyalty to His Majesty's Government, for whom he was working. Some of the songs composed in these final years, like the famous 'A man's a man for a' that', reveal his sympathy for the French people's cause and his distaste for the ruling classes.

Unfortunately for Burns and several other democratic idealists, the revolutionaries in France soon turned their attentions beyond their own country and, in February of 1793, they declared war on Britain. Coming two months after an official inquiry into his loyalty to his King, this action caused Burns a great deal of embarrassment and heightened his patriotic feelings.

The last few years of his life passed without further great upset. He continued to be distressed by the inequalities of the life he saw around him and was uncomfortable about the double life he had to lead:

half the passionate lover of romance and the folk traditions of his country, a poetic genius of international reputation, and the other half the rough-garbed ex-farmer and Exciseman, small-town husband to an ever faithful wife who was to bear him nine children, the last of these on the day of his funeral.

Burns' House at Dumfries, where he died at the age of 37.

In 1796, while still at work on the *Select Scottish Airs*, he fell seriously ill; even on his deathbed, he composed a song, 'Oh, Wert Thou in the Cauld Blast', to a moving tune he heard being played by his elderly nurse, Jessie Lewars. On 21 July, he died.

His Death

What did he leave behind?

In a Scotland of an earlier age, the genius of Robert Burns might not have burned so brightly. A wealthier and more educated society, one which was more willing to look after its poets and one in which the Church was becoming less powerful, was the society into which he was born.

Scotland after his death exploded with new industrial activity and changed completely from the country he had known. The people were becoming more accustomed to city life and, more than ever before, to the use of the English language; these had been two creative influences which had never made Burns comfortable.

The poets who followed him tried to imitate him in the style and content of their verses. They never matched him. What made Burns a poetic genius? He was more than a lover of nature who could make words dance. He had a keen eye and a great love for rural landscapes peopled and haunted by a vast celebration of life. He had a gift for writing songs which he put to work in the service of the Scottish folk tradition as no man before or since. Songs like 'Auld Lang Syne', are known around the world.

He had a fine satiric eye, a sensitivity to meanness and hypocrisy in others and a courageous sense of right and wrong. Though he used the talent only once at length, he also showed a flair for telling a story in verse. His alertness to detail, when combined with his great concern for fellow creatures of all sizes, produced poems like 'To A Mouse'.

Taken together, these talents made for a great man and a poet of stature. In seeing him as a Scottish poet, however, it is important to recognise one simple fact: he was inspired by both Scottish and English traditions that had gone before, but his poems and songs sprang from his own circumstances. In his poetry, all these influences can be working together to produce his own very individual style.

Tamas McDonald

Top *Silhouette of Burns by Miers. Miers was a very popular silhouettist, and could complete a likeness in two minutes. Burns regarded the portrait as more like him than any other.*

Left *Portrait of Burns by Peter Taylor. This painting is reputed to be the first undertaken of the poet.*

The Poetry of Robert Burns

Burns was educated in English literature from Shakespeare to his own time. He was also taught to write the correct English written by educated Englishmen. Among his friends and fellow workers in the Ayrshire countryside he spoke Ayrshire Scots. He also heard Scottish songs, ballads, folk-tales and stories sung and told all around him. As for Scottish literature, although he never heard about it from his teacher, John Murdoch, he knew some of it from the collection of older Scottish poetry called *The Ever-Green* published by Allan Ramsay in 1724, and he was very excited to discover the Scots poems of the Edinburgh poet Robert Fergusson who had died in the city in 1774 at the early age of 24. So these are what he had to draw on when he started to write his own poetry: English poetry and the English language; his native Ayrshire Scots; Scottish folk-song and folk-lore; some older Scottish poetry; and Fergusson's Scots poems. Later, when he travelled around Scotland to learn more about the places and traditions of his country, he heard the spoken Scots of a number of different parts of Scotland which he could also draw on.

The language of Burns's poetry shows all these influences. Sometimes he writes in elegant 18th-century literary English. Sometimes he writes in Scots tipped with English and sometimes in English tipped with Scots. He resisted the temptation to become an English poet writing chiefly for an English audience (as other Scottish poets of his century had done) and in his best poems moved with confidence among the various traditions available to him, gaining something from each yet giving a genuine Scottish flavour to what he wrote. He was a tenant farmer, and his experience of life gave him an intimate knowledge of the life of a peasant working in the changing seasons throughout the year, of the hardships, the joys, the friendships, the loves, of ordinary folk. From his early years Burns was also very much aware of the conflict within the Kirk between rigid Calvinists, who believed that every individual had been predestined by God since before the beginning of time to be either saved or damned (with the large majority predestined to damnation) and the 'Moderates', who believed in the importance of the 'good heart' and insisted that kindness, sympathy and tolerance in human relations rather than adherence to orthodox doctrine were the true religious virtues. Burns also bitterly resented the difference between social classes. As a youngster he played with the sons of landowners but he knew that when he and they grew up he would have to doff his cap to them as superior 'gentlemen' because they had land and money and he had not, even though they might be his inferiors in character and intelligence. All his life Burns bitterly resented the fact that a person was respected according to his rank and his money, not according to his real self. He believed that 'a man's a man for a' that'.

These three things—his knowledge of the rhythms of life of the ordinary farm worker, his belief in the importance of the 'good heart' rather than in orthodox doctrine and his passionate sense of human equality that cut across differences of rank and wealth—provide the main themes of his poetry. Burns was a great satirist, attacking or mocking or laughing at the cruelties and vanities and idiocies he saw around him. In 'Holy Willie's Prayer' he shows how a man can expose the awfulness of the creed he believes in without for a moment realising that that is what he is doing. Holy Willie is addressing God, congratulating himself that he is one of God's predestined elect so that whatever he does cannot affect his ultimate salvation. Burns makes no comment. Everything in the poem is said by Holy Willie, who condemns himself as he speaks while imagining that he is praying. This is what is known as a 'dramatic monologue', a form of poetry in which the poet puts himself in the position of somebody else and speaks in that person's character. Robert Browning and T. S. Eliot both wrote dramatic monologues, but Burns had been there before them.

Burns's satire was not always as fierce as in 'Holy Willie's Prayer'. In the 'Address to the Unco Guid' he speaks in his own person and gives us in lively and skilful verse his account of his own creed that he placed against that of the censorious and self-righteous. In 'The Twa Dogs' he uses an old Scottish tradition of animal poetry to expose the vanity and selfishness of the lives of certain kinds of idle rich, in opposition to the life of the poor which, though often harsh, has its warm human compensations. The rich man's dog, in his knowing description of his master's way of life, is really exposing its awfulness, while the poor man's dog speaks for the poet. It is all done with artfulness and humour.

Burns uses the old Scottish tradition of animal poetry in other ways too, showing the farmer's feelings for his farm animals as fellow workers in a hard world and even, in the famous 'To a Mouse' (written in a favourite old Scots stanza form), showing sympathy for the unfortunate little creature whose house and livelihood are threatened by the plough, just as Burns's own livelihood was threatened by other kinds of misfortune. This feeling for animals is not sentimental; it is grounded in the genuine experience of a farmer working in a Scottish agricultural scene.

'To a Mouse' — Burns at the plough turning up the mouse, by Gowley Steell engraved by John le Conte.

Burns had a great gift for friendship, and this shows itself in his verse letters or 'epistles'. This is a difficult kind of poetry to write, for it requires the informal tone of a letter to a friend at the same time as it uses rhyme and metre with careful craftmanship. His verse letters generally begin by setting the scene, giving the season of the year (so important to a farmer) and the feel of the countryside, then moving on to make some general statement about life or love or poetry or some other large general subject before coming back again to himself writing in the farmhouse kitchen and then signing off. He could address animals and inanimate objects as well as friends, but this was in a different kind of poetry as in the exaggerated humorous celebration of 'To a Haggis' or the mock indignation of 'To a Louse' where the proud girl with her new bonnet in church is gently laughed at for her pretensions, which are mocked by the louse that crawls on it without her knowing it. In the 'Address to the Deil' Burns reduces the formidable Enemy of Mankind, thundered about so threateningly in the pulpit, to the level of a mischievous schoolboy who perhaps in the end might repent and be saved (an appalling thought to the orthodox).

Burns wrote one great narrative poem, 'Tam O' Shanter', based on a local folk story. Here he shows his mastery of the eight-syllable couplet, his ability to change the speed and tone of the verse as it moves from description of the cosy pub interior to the howling gale outside or as it alters from direct description to mock moralising.

Perhaps Burns's most loved poems are his songs. He set himself the task of re-creating the mass of half-forgotten Scottish folk-song. Sometimes a chorus survived without the verses; sometimes the tune without the words; often a fragment or an odd stanza or a tag line. Writing always with a particular tune in mind—for Burns was a genius at writing words to an existing tune—he improved, revised, re-wrote, completed or invented hundreds of folk-songs, very often not claiming the result as his own, but saying that he got it from the singing of some old man or other country character. Sometimes he builds up a

Tam o' Shanter racing to safety on his grey mare Meg, over the Brig o' Doon, with the young witch in her cutty sark hanging onto Meg's tail.

poem by taking surviving lines, perhaps from different songs, and arranging them in a special way or surrounding them with lines of his own or in some other way giving new life and emotional power to old fragments (he did this, for example, in 'A red, red rose' and 'Auld Lang Syne'). He could sing of love, either of a man for a girl or of a girl for a man, or friendship ('Auld Lang Syne' is the great poem of remembered friendship), of work and play, of local scenes and celebrations. At the centre is always the human emotion; though he could describe the Scottish landscape with moving accuracy, his landscapes are always landscapes with figures: it is the *people* and their feelings that count. The songs are sometimes passionate, sometimes humorous, sometimes looking back to the lost causes of history ('It was a' for our rightfu' King'), sometimes patriotic ('Scots wha hae'), sometimes picking up and restoring a fragmentary work song he found coming, say, from the fisher folk of Fife ('Hey ca' thro'), sometimes laughing at himself ('There was a Lad'), sometimes hauntingly protective of the girl he is speaking to ('O, wert Thou in the Cauld Blast'), sometimes setting a love scene with beautifully moving detail in a particular time and place ('The Lea-rig'). We must remember always that these are *songs*, to be fully appreciated only when sung to their tunes. 'Ay Waukin' O', 'Ca' the Yowes', 'The Banks o' Doon' and 'O, Whistle an' I'll come to ye, my Lad'

An engraving by John Faed of 'The Cotter's Saturday Night'.

are examples of songs that lose an enormous amount when just read as poems. In the songs we are vividly presented with the feelings of men and women at work and at play generally in the farmer's world of seasonal change.

David Daiches

The Jolly Beggars

Animal Poems

The Death and Dying Words of Poor Mailie

The Author's Only Pet Yowe: an Unco Mournfu' Tale

As Mailie, an' her lambs thegither,   Mollie; together
Was ae day nibbling on the tether.   one
Upon her cloot she coost a hitch,   hoof; looped
An' owre she warsl'd in the ditch: floundered
There, groaning, dying, she did lie,
When Hughoc he cam doytan by.   doddering

Wi' glowrin een, an' lifted han's   staring
Poor Hughoc like a statue stan's;
He saw her days were near-hand ended,
But, wae's my heart! he could na mend it!   woe
He gapèd wide, but naething spak.
At length poor Mailie silence brak:

'O thou, whase lamentable face
Appears to mourn my woefu' case!
My dying words attentive hear,
An' bear them to my Master dear.

'Tell him, if e'er again he keep   own
As muckle gear as buy a sheep   much money
O, bid him never tie them mair,
Wi' wicked strings o' hemp or hair!
But ca' them out to park or hill,   drive
An' let them wander at their will:
So may his flock increase, an' grow
To scores o' lambs, an' packs o' woo'!

'Tell him, he was a Master kin',
An' ay was guid to me an' mine;
An' now my dying charge I gie him,
My helpless lambs, I trust them wi' him.

'O, bid him save their harmless lives,
Frae dogs, an' tods, an' butchers' knives!   foxes
But gie them guid cow-milk their fill,
Till they be fit to fend themsel;   look after
An' tent them duly, e'en an' morn,   tend
Wi' teats o' hay an' ripps o' corn.   small quantities; handfuls

'An' may they never learn the gaets   ways
Of ither vile, wanrestfu' pets,   restless
To slink thro' slaps, an' reave an' steal,   breaches
At stacks o' pease, or stocks o' kail.
So may they, like their great forbears,
For monie a year come thro' the sheers:
So wives will gie them bits o' bread
An' bairns greet for them when they're dead.   weep

'My poor toop-lamb, my son an' heir,
O, bid him breed him up wi' care!
An' if he live to be a beast,
To pit some havins in his breast!
An' warn him — what I winnae name —
To stay content wi' yowes at hame;
An' no to rin an' wear his cloots,
Like other menseless, graceless brutes.

'An' niest, my yowie, silly thing,
Gude keep thee frae a tether string!
O, may thou ne'er forgather up,
Wi' onie blastit, moorland toop;
But ay keep mind to moop an' mell,
Wi' sheep o' credit like thysel!

'And now, my bairns, wi' my last breath,
I lea'e my blessin wi' you baith:
An' when you think upo' your mither,
Mind to be kind to ane anither.

'Now, honest Hughoc, dinna fail,
To tell my master a' my tale;
An' bid him burn this cursèd tether,
An' for thy pains thou'se get my blether.'

This said, poor Mailie turn'd her head,
An' clos'd her een amang the dead!

Glossary (left margin):
- tup (ram)
- behaviour
- will not
- ewes
- unmannerly
- ewekin; helpless
- make friends
- nibble; meddle
- bladder
- eyes

Poor Mailie's Elegy

Lament in rhyme, lament in prose,
Wi' saut tears tricklin down your nose;
Our Bardie's fate is at a close,
                    Past a' remead!
The last, sad cape-stane of his woes;
                    Poor Mailie's dead!

It's no the loss of warl's gear,
That could sae bitter draw the tear,
Or mak our Bardie, dowie, wear
                    The mourning weed:
He's lost a friend an' neebor dear
                    In Mailie dead.

Glossary (left margin):
- remedy
- worldy goods
- sad

Thro' a' the toun she trotted by him;   farm
A lang half-mile she could descry him;
Wi' kindly bleat, when she did spy him,
                    She ran wi' speed:
A friend mair faithfu' ne'er cam nigh him,
                    Than Mailie dead.

I wat she was a sheep o' sense,   wot
An' could behave hersel wi' mense: tact
I'll say 't, she never brak a fence,
                    Thro' thievish greed.
Our Bardie, lanely, keeps the spence   parlour
                    Sin' Mailie's dead.

Or, if he wanders up the howe,   glen
Her livin image in her yowe   ewe
Comes bleatin till him, owrè the knowe,   knoll
                    For bits o' bread;
An' down the briny pearls rowe   roll
                    For Mailie dead.

She was nae get o' moorlan tips,   issue; tups (rams)
Wi' tawted ket, an' hairy hips;   matted fleece; rumps
For her forbears were brought in ships,
                    Frae 'yont the Tweed:
A bonier fleesh ne'er cross'ed the clips   fleece; shears
                    Than Mailie's dead.

Wae worth the man wha first did shape   Woe befall
That vile, wanchancie thing — a rape!   dangerous
It maks guid fellows girn an' gape,   snarl in agony
                    Wi' chokin dread;
An' Robin's bonnet wave wi' crape
                    For Mailie dead.

O a' ye bards on bonie Doon!
An' wha on Ayr your chanters tune!   bagpipes
Come, join the melancholious croon
                    O' Robin's reed!
His heart will never get aboon!   rejoice
                    His Mailie's dead!

To a Mouse

On Turning Her up in Her Nest with the Plough, November 1785

Wee, sleekit, cowran, tim'rous beastie,   sleek
O, what a panic's in thy breastie!
Thou need na start awa sae hasty
                    Wi' bickering brattle!   hurrying scamper
I wad be laith to rin an' chase thee,   loth
                    Wi' murdering pattle!   long-handled spade

45

I'm truly sorry man's dominion
Has broken Nature's social union,
An' justifies that ill opinion
                    Which makes thee startle
At me, thy poor, earth-born companion
                    An' fellow mortal!

sometimes   I doubt na, whyles, but thou may thieve;
must   What then? poor beastie, thou maun live!
odd ear; twenty-four   A daimen icker in a thrave
sheaves   'S a sma' request;
remainder   I'll get a blessin wi' the lave,
                    An' never miss't!

feeble; winds   Thy wee-bit housie, too, in ruin!
    Its silly wa's the win's are strewin!
build   An' naething, now, to big a new ane,
coarse grass   O' foggage green!
    An' bleak December's win's ensuin,
bitter   Baith snell an' keen!

Thou saw the fields laid bare an' waste,
An' weary winter comin fast,
An' cozie here, beneath the blast,
                    Thou thought to dwell,
Till crash! the cruel coulter past
                    Out thro' thy cell.

stubble   That wee bit heap o' leaves an' stibble,
    Has cost thee monie a weary nibble!
    Now thou's turned out, for a' thy trouble,
Without; holding   But house or hald,
endure   To thole thy winter's sleety dribble,
hoar-frost   An' cranreuch cauld!

alone   But Mousie, thou art no thy lane,
    In proving foresight may be vain:
    The best-laid schemes o' mice an' men
askew   Gang aft agley,
    An' lea'e us nought but grief an' pain,
                    For promis'd joy!

Still, thou art blest, compared wi' me!
The present only toucheth thee:
But och! I backward cast my e'e,
                    On prospects drear!
An' forward, tho' I canna see,
                    I guess an' fear!

The Auld Farmer's New-Year Morning Salutation to His Auld Mare, Maggie

On Giving Her the Accustomed Ripp of Corn to Hansel in the New-Year

A Guid New-Year I wish thee, Maggie!
Hae, there's a ripp to thy auld baggie: *handful of unthreshed corn; belly*
Tho' thou's howe-backit now, an' knaggie,   *hollow-backed; knobby*
           I've seen the day
Thou could hae gaen like onie staggie,   *gone; colt*
           Out-owre the lay.   *beyond; lea*

Tho' now thou's dowie, stiff, an' crazy   *dejected*
An' thy auld hide as white's a daisie,
I've seen thee dappl't, sleek an' glaizie,   *shiny*
           A bonie gray:
He should been tight that daur't to raize thee,   *prepared; excite*
           Ance in a day.

Thou ance was i' the foremost rank,
A filly buirdly, steeve, an' swank: *stalwart, firm and agile*
An' set weel down a shapely shank
           As e'er tread yird;   *earth*
An' could hae flown out-owre a stank   *pond*
           Like onie bird.

It's now some nine-an'-twenty year
Sin' thou was my guid-father's meere;   *father-in-law's*
He gied me thee, o' tocher clear,   *wholly as dowry*
           An' fifty mark;
Tho' it was sma', 'twas weel-won gear,
           An' thou was stark.   *strong*

When first I gaed to woo my Jenny,   *went*
Ye then was trottan wi' your minnie: *mother*
Tho' ye was trickie, slee, an' funnie,   *sly*
           Ye ne'er was donsie: *mischievous*
But hamely, tawie, quiet, an' cannie,   *tractable*
           An' unco sonsie.   *good-tempered*

That day, ye pranc'd wi' muckle pride,
When ye bure hame my bonie bride: *bore*
An' sweet an' gracefu' she did ride,
           Wi' maiden air!
Kyle-Stewart I could braggèd wide,   *have challenged*
           For sic a pair.

47

can; stumble
stagger; salmon-boat
goer
wind
wobble

Tho' now ye dow but hoyte and hobble,
An' wintle like a saumont-coble,
That day, ye was a jinker noble,
      For heels an' win'!
An' ran them till they a' did wauble,
      Far, far behin'!

skittish
tedious
snort; whinny

aloof

When thou an' I were young and skiegh,
An' stable-meals at fairs were driegh,
How thou wad prance, an' snore, an' skriegh,
      An' tak the road!
Town's-bodies ran, an' stood abiegh,
      An' ca't thee mad.

When thou was corn't, an' I was mellow,
We took the road ay like a swallow:
wedding-races
At brooses thou had ne'er a fellow,
      For pith an' speed;
But ev'ry tail thou pay't them hollow,
      Whare're thou gaed.

short-rumped
perhaps have beat;
spurt
wheeze

willow

The sma, droop-rumpl't, hunter cattle
Might aiblins waur't thee for a brattle;
But sax Scotch miles thou try't their mettle,
      An' gar't them whaizle:
Nae whip nor spur, but just a wattle
      O' saugh or hazle.

near left-hand horse in
the plough
going

by ourselves

Thou was a noble fittie-lan',
As e'er in tug or tow was drawn!
Aft thee an' I, in aught hours' gaun,
      On guid March-weather,
Hae turn'd sax rood beside our han'
      For days thegither.

drew unsteadily;
stopped suddenly;
fretted
rushy hillocks would
have roared; cracked
fallen smoothly over

Thou never braing't, an' fetch't, an' fliskit;
But thy auld tail thou wad hae whiskit,
An' spread abreed thy weel-fill'd brisket,
      Wi' pith an' pow'r;
Till sprittie knowes wad rair't, an' riskit,
      An' slypet owre.

When frosts lay lang, an' snaws were deep,
An' threaten'd labour back to keep,
dish
I gied thy cog a wee bit heap
edge
      Aboon the timmer:
I ken'd my Maggie wad na sleep
ere
      For that, or simmer.

In cart or car thou never reestit;
stiffest incline
The steyest brae thou wad hae fac't it;
leaped; sprang
Thou never lap, an' sten't, an' breastit,
      Then stood to blaw;
But just thy step a wee thing hastit,
jogged along
      Thou snoov't awa.

My pleugh is now thy bairntime a',   team; offspring
Four gallant brutes as e'er did draw;
Forby sax mae I've sell't awa,   more
                    That thou hast nurst:
They drew me thretteen pund an' twa,
                    The vera warst.

Monie a sair darg we twa hae wrought,   day's work
An' wi' the weary warl' fought!
An' monie an anxious day I thought
                    We wad be beat!
Yet here to crazy age we're brought,
                    Wi' something yet.

An' think na, my auld trusty servan',
That now perhaps thou's less deservin,
An' thy auld days may end in starvin;
                    For my last fow,   bushel
A heapet stimpart, I'll reserve ane   quarter-peck
                    Laid by for you.

We've worn to crazy years thegither;
We'll toyte about wi' ane anither;   totter
Wi' tentie care I'll flit thy tether   change
                    To some hain'd rig,   reserved patch
Whare ye may nobly rax your leather   fill your stomach
                    Wi' sma' fatigue.

49

Satires

Address to the Unco Guid

or the Rigidly Righteous

My Son, these maxims make a rule,
    An' lump them ay thegither:
The Rigid Righteous is a fool,
    The Rigid Wise anither;
sifted   *The cleanest corn that e'er was dight*
chaff   *May hae some pyles o' caff in;*
So ne'er a fellow-creature slight
fun   *For random fits o' daffin.*
SOLOMON *(Eccles.* vii. 16)

O ye wha are sae guid yoursel,
    Sae pious and sae holy,
Ye've nought to do but mark and tell
    Your neebours' fauts and folly!
well-going   Whase life is like a weel-gaun mill,
    Supplied wi' store o' water;
heaped hopper   The heapet happer's ebbing still,
clapper   An' still the clap plays clatter.

company   Hear me, ye venerable core,
    As counsel for poor mortals
sober   That frequent pass douce Wisdom's door
giddy   For glaikit Folly's portals:
I, for their thoughtless, careless sakes
propose   Would here propone defences,
unlucky   Their donsie tricks, their black mistakes,
    Their failings and mischances.

Ye see your state wi' theirs compared,
difference   And shudder at the niffer;
But cast a moment's fair regard,
    What makes the mighty differ?
Discount what scant occasion gave,
    That purity ye pride in;
rest   And (what's aft mair than a' the lave)
    Your better art o' hidin.

50

Think, when your castigated pulse
   Gies now and then a wallop,
What ragings must his veins convulse
   That still eternal gallop:
Wi' wind and tide fair i' your tail
   Right on ye scud your sea-way;
But in the teeth o' baith to sail,
   It makes an unco lee-way.   strange

See Social-life and Glee sit down
   All joyous and unthinking,
Till, quite transmugrify'd, they're grown
   Debauchery and Drinking:
O, would they stay to calculate,
   Th' eternal consequences,
Or, your more dreaded hell to state,
   Damnation of expenses!

Ye high, exalted, virtuous dames,
   Tied up in godly laces,
Before ye gie poor Frailty names,
   Suppose a change o' cases:
A dear-lov'd lad, convenience snug,
   A treach'rous inclination —
But, let me whisper i' your lug,   ear
   Ye're aiblins nae temptation.   maybe

Then gently scan your brother man,
   Still gentler sister woman;
Tho' they may gang a kennin wrang,
   To step aside is human:
One point must still be greatly dark,
   The moving *why* they do it;
And just as lamely can ye mark
   How far perhaps they rue it.

Who made the heart, 'tis He alone
   Decidedly can try us:
He knows each chord its various tone,
   Each spring its various bias:
Then at the balance let's be mute,
   We never can adjust it;
What's *done* we partly may compute,
   But know not what's *resisted*.

Holy Willie's Prayer

And send the godly in a pet to pray.

Argument

Holy Willie was a rather oldish bachelor Elder in the parish of
Mauchline, and much and justly famed for that polemical
chattering which ends in tippling orthodoxy, and for the
spiritualized bawdry which refines to liquorish devotion. In a
sessional process with a gentleman of Mauchline, a Mr Gavin
Hamilton, Holy Willie, and his priest, Father Auld, after full
hearing in the Presbytery of Ayr, came off second best, owing
partly to the rhetorical powers of Mr Robt. Aiken, Mr
Hamilton's Counsel, but chiefly to Mr Hamilton's being one of
the most irreproachable and truly respectable characters in the
country. On losing his process, the Muse overheard him in his
devotions as follows. (Burns's headnote.)

O Thou that in the Heavens does dwell,
Wha, as it pleases best thysel,
Sends ane to Heaven an' ten to Hell
      A' for thy glory,
And no for onie guid or ill
      They've done before Thee.

I bless and praise thy matchless might,
When thousands thou has left in night,
That I am here before thy sight,
      For gifts an' grace
A burning and a shining light
      To a' this place.

such   What was I, or my generation,
That I should get sic exaltation?
I, wha deserv'd most just damnation
      For broken laws
Six   Sax thousand years ere my creation,
      Thro' Adam's cause!

When from my mither's womb I fell,
Thou might hae plung'd me deep in hell
gums   To gnash my gooms, and weep, and wail
      In burning lakes,
Whare damnèd devils roar and yell,
      Chain'd to their stakes.

Yet I am here, a chosen sample,
To show thy grace is great and ample:
I'm here, a pillar o' thy temple,
      Strong as a rock,
A guide, a buckler, and example
      To a' thy flock!

But yet, O Lord, confess I must:
At times I'm fash'd wi' fleshly lust;   troubled
An' sometimes, too, in wardly trust,
        Vile self gets in;
But Thou remembers we are dust,
        Defil'd wi' sin.

O Lord, yestreen, thou kens, wi' Meg —   last night; knowest
Thy pardon I sincerely beg!
O, may't ne'er be a living plague
        To my dishonour!
An' I'll ne'er lift a lawless leg
        Again upon her.

Besides, I farther maun avow —   must
Wi' Leezie's lass, three times, I trow —
But, Lord, that Friday I was fou   drunk
        When I cam near her,
Or else, thou kens, thy servant true
        Wad never steer her.   Would; disturb

Maybe thou lets this fleshy thorn
Buffet thy servant e'en and morn
Lest he owre proud and high should turn   too
        That he's sae gifted;
If sae, thy han' maun e'en be borne
        Until thou lift it.

Lord, bless thy chosen in this place,
For here thou has a chosen race:
But God, confound their stubborn face
        An' blast their name,
Wha bring thy elders to disgrace
        An' open shame!

Lord, mind Gau'n Hamilton's deserts:
He drinks, an' swears, an' plays at cartes,   cards
Yet has sae monie takin arts
        Wi' great and sma',
Frae God's ain priest the people's hearts
        He steals awa.

And when we chasten'd him therefore,
Thou kens how he bred sic a splore,   uproar
And set the warld in a roar
        O' laughing at us:
Curse thou his basket and his store,
        Kail an' potatoes!   Cabbage

Lord, hear my earnest cry and pray'r
Against that Presbyt'ry of Ayr!
Thy strong right hand, Lord mak it bare
        Upo' their heads!
do not   Lord, visit them, an' dinna spare,
        For their misdeeds!

O Lord, my God! that glibe-tongu'd Aiken!
My vera heart and flesh are quakin
To think how we stood sweatin, shakin,
        An' piss'd wi' dread,
sneering   While he, wi' hingen lip an' sneakin,
        Held up his head.

Lord, in thy day o' vengeance try him!
Lord, visit him wha did employ him!
And pass not in thy mercy by them,
        Nor hear their pray'r,
But for thy people's sake destroy them,
        An'dinna spare!

But, Lord, remember me and mine
Wi' mercies temporal and divine,
wealth   That I for grace an' gear may shine,
        Excell'd by nane;
And a' the glory shall be Thine!
        Amen, Amen!

The Twa Dogs

A Tale

'Twas in that place o' Scotland's isle
That bears the name of auld King Coil,*
Upon a bonie day in June,
When wearing thro' the afternoon,
busy   Twa dogs, that were nae thrang at hame,
got together   Forgathered ance upon a time.

    The first I'll name, they ca'd him Caesar,
Was keepit for his Honor's pleasure:
ears   His hair, his size, his mouth, his lugs,
Shew'd he was nane o' Scotland's dogs;
But whalpit some place far abroad,
Whare sailors gang to fish for cod.

* Kyle, the middle district of Ayrshire.

54

His lockèd, letter'd, braw brass collar
Shew'd him the gentleman an' scholar;
But tho' he was o' high degree,
The fient a pride, nae pride had he;   *The devil a bit of pride*
But wad hae spent an hour caressan,
Ev'n wi' a tinkler-gipsy's messan;   *mongrel*
At kirk or market, mill or smiddie,   *smithy*
Nae tawted tyke, tho' e'er sae duddie,   *matted cur; ragged*
But he wad stan't, as glad to see him,   *would have stood*
An' stroan't on stanes an' hillocks wi' him.   *pissed*

   The tither was a ploughman's collie,
A rhyming, ranting, raving billie,   *rollicking fellow*
Wha for his friend an' comrade had him,
And in his freaks had Luath ca'd him,
After some dog in Highland sang,†
Was made lang syne — Lord knows how lang.

   He was a gash an' faithfu' tyke,   *wise*
As ever lap a sheugh or dyke.   *ditch; stone fence*
His honest, sonsie, baws'nt face   *pleasant, white-streaked*
Ay gat him friends in ilka place;   *every*
His breast was white, his touzie back   *shaggy*
Weel clad wi' coat o' glossy black;
His gawsie tail, wi' upward curl,   *joyous*
Hung owre his hurdies wi' a swirl.   *buttocks*

   Nae doubt but they were fain o' ither,   *fond of each other*
And unco pack an' thick thegither;   *confidential*
Wi'social nose whyles snuff'd an' snowkit;   *now*
Whyles mice an' moudieworts they howkit;   *moles; dug*
Whyles scour'd awa' in lang excursion,
An' worry'd ither in diversion;
Till tir'd at last wi' monie a farce,
They sat them down upon their arse,
An' there began a lang digression
About the 'lords o' the creation.'

CAESAR

   I've aften wonder'd, honest Luath,
What sort o' life poor dogs like you have;
An' when the gentry's life I saw,
What way poor bodies liv'd ava.   *at all*

† Cuchullin's dog in Ossian's 'Fingal'. (Burns's note.)

55

Our laird gets in his rackèd rents,
His coals, his kane, an' a' his stents: *rents in kind; dues*
He rises when he likes himsel;
His flunkies answer at the bell;
He ca's his coach; he ca's his horse;
He draws a bonie silken purse,
As lang's my tail, where, thro' the steeks, *stitches*
The yellow, letter'd Geordie keeks. *guinea peeps*

Frae morn to e'en it's nought but toiling,
At baking, roasting, frying, boiling;
An' tho' the gentry first are stechin, *cramming*
Yet ev'n the ha' folk fill their peghan *servants; stomach*
Wi' sauce, ragouts, an sic like trashtrie,
That's little short o' downright wastrie:
Our whipper-in, wee, blastit wonner,
Poor, worthless elf, it eats a dinner,
Better than onie tenant-man
His Honour has in a' the lan';
An' what poor cot-folk pit in their painch in, *put; paunch*
I own it's past my comprehension.

LUATH

Trowth, Caesar, whyles they're fash't eneugh: *sometimes; bothered*
A cotter howkan in a sheugh, *digging*
Wi' dirty stanes biggan a dyke, *building*
Bairan a quarry, an' sic like; *clearing*
Himsel, a wife, he thus sustains,
A smytrie o' wee duddie weans, *litter; ragged kids*
An' nought but his han'-darg to keep *hands' labour*
Them right an' tight in thack an' rape. *thatch and rope*
An' when they meet wi' sair disasters
Like loss o' health or want o' masters,
Ye maist wad think, a wee touch langer, *small*
An' they maun starve o' cauld and hunger: *must*
But how it comes, I never kent yet,
They're maistly wonderfu' contented;
An' buirdly chiels, an' clever hizzies, *stout lads; young women*
Are bred in sic a way as this is.

CAESAR

But then to see how ye're negleckit,
How huff'd, an' cuff'd, an' disrepseckit!
Lord man, our gentry care as little
For delvers, ditchers, an' sic cattle;
They gang as saucy by poor folk,
As I wad by a stinkan brock. *badger*

I've notic'd, on our laird's court-day,
(An' monie a time my heart's been wae),   sad
Poor tenant bodies, scant o' cash,
How they maun thole a factor's snash: endure; abuse
He'll stamp an' threaten, curse an' swear,
He'll apprehend them, poind their gear;   seize
While they maun staun', wi' aspect humble,   stand
An' hear it a', an' fear an' tremble!

I see how folk live that hae riches;
But surely poor-folk maun be wretches!

LUATH

They're nae sae wretched's ane wad think:
Tho' constantly on poortith's brink,   poverty's
They're sae accustom'd wi' the sight,
The view o't gies them little fright.

Then chance an' fortune are sae guided,
They're ay in less or mair provided;
An' tho' fatigu'd wi' close employment,
A blink o' rest's a sweet enjoyment.   snatch

The dearest comfort o' their lives,
Their grushie weans an' faithfu' wives;   growing
The prattling things are just their pride,
That sweetens a' their fire-side.

An' whyles twalpennie worth o' nappy   sometimes; ale
Can mak the bodies unco happy:
They lay aside their private cares,
To mind the Kirk an' State affairs;
They'll talk o' patronage an' priests,
Wi' kindling fury i' their breasts,
Or tell what new taxation's comin,
An' ferlie at the folk in Lon'on.   marvel

As bleak-fac'd Hallowmass returns,
They get the jovial, rantan kirns,   harvest-homes
When rural life, of ev'ry station,
Unite in common recreation;
Love blinks, Wit slaps, an' social Mirth   glances
Forgets there's Care upo' the earth.

That merry day the year begins,
They bar the door on frosty win's;
The nappy reeks wi' mantling ream,   foaming froth
An' sheds a heart-inspiring steam;
The luntin pipe, an' sneeshin mill,   smoking; snuff box
Are handed round wi' right guid will:
The cantie auld folks crackan crouse,   conversing cheerfully
The young anes rantan thro' the house —   romping
My heart has been sae fain to see them,
That I for joy hae barkit wi' them.

Still it's owre true that ye hae said

too often   Sic game is now owre aften play'd;
There's monie a creditable stock

respectable   O' decent, honest, fawsont folk,
Are riven out baith root an' branch,
Some rascal's pridefu' greed to quench,
Wha thinks to knit himsel the faster
In favour wi' some gentle master,

maybe busy   Wha, aiblins thrang a parliamentin',
indenturing   For Britain's guid his saul indentin' —

CAESAR

Haith lad, ye little ken about it:
For Britain's guid! guid faith! I doubt it.

going   Say rather, gaun as Premiers lead him,
An' saying *aye* or *no*'s they bid him:
At operas an' plays parading,
Mortgaging, gambling, masquerading:
Or maybe, in a frolic daft,
To Hague or Calais taks a waft,
To mak a tour an' tak a whirl,
To learn *bon ton*, an' see the worl'.

There, at Vienna or Versailles,

breaks up   He rives his father's auld entails;
road   Or by Madrid he taks the rout,
fight; cattle   To thrum guitars an' fecht wi' nowt;
Or down Italian vista startles,
Whore-hunting amang groves o' myrtles:

muddy   Then bowses drumlie German-water,
To mak himself look fair an' fatter,

sores   An' purge the bitter ga's an' cankers
venereal sores   O' curst Venetian bores an' chancres.

For Britain's guid! for her destruction!
Wi' dissipation, leud an' faction.

LUATH

way   Hech man! dear sirs! is that the gate
They waste sae monie a braw estate!

troubled   Are we sae foughten an' harass'd
wealth to go   For gear ta gang that gate at last?

O would they stay aback frae courts,
An' please themsels wi' countra sports,
It wad for ev'ry ane be better,
The laird, the tenant, an' the cotter!
For thae frank, rantin, ramblin billies, *those; roistering*
Fient haet o' them's ill-hearted fellows: *Not one*
Except for breakin o' their timmer, *wasting their woods*
Or speakin lightly o' their limmer, *mistress*
Or shootin of a hare or moor-cock,
The ne'er-a-bit they're ill to poor folk.

But will ye tell me, master Caesar:
Sure great folk's life's a life o' pleasure?
Nae could nor hunger e'er can steer them,
The vera thought o't need na fear them. *touch*

CAESAR

Lord, man, were ye but whyles whare I am,
The gentles, ye wad ne'er envý em!

It's true, they need na starve or sweat,
Thro' winter's cauld, or simmer's heat;
They've nae sair wark to craze their banes, *hard*
An' fill auld-age wi' grips an' granes: *gripes and groans*
But human bodies are sic fools,
For a' their colleges an' schools,
That when nae *real* ills perplex them,
They *mak* enow themsels to vex them, *fret*
An' ay the less they hae to sturt them,
In like proprtion, less will hurt them.

A countra fellow at the pleugh,
His acre's till'd, he's right eneugh;
A countra girl at her wheel,
Her dizzen's done, she's unco weel; *dozen*
But gentlemen, an' ladies warst,
Wi' ev'n down want o' wark are curst: *positive*
They loiter, lounging, lank an' lazy;
Tho' deil-haet ails them, yet uneasy: *nothing*
Their days insipid, dull an' tasteless;
Their nights unquiet, lang an' restless.

An' ev'n their sports, their balls an' races
Their galloping through public places,
There's sic parade, sic pomp an' art,
The joy can scarcely reach the heart.

The men cast out in party-matches,
Then sowther a' in deep debauches; *solder*
Ae night they're mad wi' drink an' whoring, *One*
Niest day their life is past enduring. *Next*

The ladies arm-in-arm in clusters,
As great an' gracious a' as sisters;
But hear their absent thoughts o' ither,
downright They're a' run deils an' jads thegither.
Whyles, owre the wee bit cup an' platie,
They sip the scandal-potion pretty;
live-long Or lee-lang nights, wi' crabbit leuks
i.e. playing cards Pore owre the devil's pictur'd beuks;
Stake on a chance a farmer's stackyard,
An' cheat like onie unhang'd blackguard.

There's some exceptions, man an' woman;
But this is Gentry's life in common.

By this, the sun was out o' sight,
twilight An' darker gloamin brought the night;
beetle The bum-clock humm'd wi' lazy drone;
cattle; lowing; side path The kye stood rowtin' i' the loan;
ears When up they gat, an' shook their lugs,
Rejoic'd they were na *men*, but *dogs*;
An' each took off his several way,
Resolv'd to meet some ither day.

Letters and addresses

Epistle to Davie, a Brother Poet

While winds frae aff Ben-Lomond blaw,
And bar the doors wi' driving snaw,
fire And hing us owre the ingle,
I set me down to pass the time,
And spin a verse or twa o' rhyme,
westland In hamely, westlin jingle:
Right to the chimney While frosty winds blaw in the drift,
corner Ben to the chimla lug,
I grudge a wee the great-folk's gift,
comfortable That live sae bien an' snug:
value I tent less, and want less
Their roomy fire-side;
But hanker, and canker,
To see their cursed pride.

It's hardly in a body's pow'r,
To keep, at times, frae being sour,
    To see how things are shar'd;
How best o' chiels are whyles in want,   *chaps; sometimes*
While coofs on countless thousands rant,   *dolts; roister*
    And ken na how to wair't;   *spend*
But David lad, ne'er fash your head,   *trouble*
    Tho' we hae little gear;   *wealth*
We're fit to win our daily bread,
    As lang's we're hale and fier: *whole; sound*
        'Mair spier na, nor fear na',*   *ask not*
            Auld age ne'er mind a feg;   *fig*
        The last o't, the warst o't,
            Is only but to beg.

To lie in kilns and barns at e'en,
When banes are craz'd, and bluid is thin,
    Is, doubtless, great distress!
Yet then content could make us blest;
Ev'n then, sometimes, we'd snatch a taste
    Of truest happiness.
The honest heart that's free frae a'
    Intended fraud or guile,
However Fortune kick the ba',
    Has ay some cause to smile;
        And mind still, you'll find still,
            A comfort this nae sma';
        Nae mair then, we'll care then,
            Nae farther can we fa'.

What tho', like commoners of air,
We wander out, we know not where,
    But either house or hal'?   *Without; holding*
Yet Nature's charms, the hills and woods,
The sweeping vales, and foaming floods,
    Are free alike to all.
In days when daisies deck the ground,
    And blackbirds whistle clear,
With honest joy our hearts will bound,
    To see the coming year:
        On braes when we please then,   *hill-sides*
            We'll sit an' sowth a tune;   *hum*
        Syne rhyme till't we'll time till't,   *Then*
            An' sing't when we hae done.

* A quotation from Allan Ramsay's 'The Poet's Wish'.

It's no in titles nor in rank:
It's no in wealth like Lon'on Bank,
  To purchase peace and rest.
It's no in makin muckle, mair; *much, more*
It's no in books, it's no in lear, *learning*
  To make us truly blest:
If happiness hae not her seat
  An' centre in the breast,
We may be wise, or rich, or great,
  But never can be blest!
    Nae treasures nor pleasures
      Could make us happy lang;
    The heart ay's the part ay
      That makes us right or wrang. . . .

Second Epistle to J. Lapraik

April 21, 1785

While new-ca'd kye rowte at the stake *new-driven; low*
An' pownies reek in pleugh or braik, *smoke; harrow*
This hour on e'enin's edge I take,
            To own I'm debtor
To honest-hearted, auld Lapraik,
            For his kind letter.

Forjesket sair, with weary legs, *Jaded*
Rattlin the corn out-owre the rigs, *ridges*
Or dealing thro' amang the naigs *distributing*
            Their ten-hours' bite,
My awkart Muse sair pleads and begs,
            I would na write.

The tapetless, ramfeezl'd hizzie, *feckless, exhausted girl*
She's saft at best an' something lazy;
Quo' she: 'Ye ken we've been sae busy
            This month an' mair,
That trowth, my head is grown right dizzie,
            An' something sair.'

Her dowff excuses pat me mad: *dull*
'Conscience,' says I, 'ye thowless jad! *lazy*
I'll write, an' that a hearty blaud, *screed*
            This vera night;
So dinna ye affront your trade, *do not*
            But rhyme it right.

'Shall bauld Lapraik, the king o' hearts,
Tho' mankind were a pack o' cartes,
Roose you sae weel for your deserts,   Praise
        In terms sae friendly;
Yet ye'll neglect to shaw your parts
        An' thank him kindly?'

Sae I gat paper in a blink   twinkling
An' down gaed stumpie in the ink:
Quoth I: 'Before I sleep a wink,
        I vow I'll close it:
An' if ye winna make it clink,   rhyme
        By Jove, I'll prose it!'

Sae I've begun to scrawl, but whether
In rhyme, or prose, or baith thegither,
Or some hotch-potch that's rightly neither,
        Let time mak proof;
But I shall scribble down some blether   nonsense
        Just clean aff-loof.   off-hand

My worthy friend, ne'er grudge an' carp,
Tho' Fortune use you hard an' sharp;
Come, kittle up your moorland harp   tickle
        Wi' gleesome touch!
Ne'er mind how Fortune waft an' warp;   woof
        She's but a bitch.

She's gien me monie a jirt an' fleg,   jerk; scare
Sin' I could striddle owre a rig;   straddle
But, by the Lord, tho' I should beg
        Wi' lyart pow,   grey head
I'll laugh an' sing, an' shake my leg,   dance
        As lang's I dow!   can

Now comes the sax-an-twentieth simmer
I've seen the bud upo' the timmer,   trees
Still persecuted by the limmer   jade
        Frae year to year;
But yet, despite the kittle kimmer,   fickle gossip
        I, Rob, am here.

Do ye envý the city gent,
Behint a kist to lie an' sklent;   counter; cheat
Or purse-proud, big wi' cent per cent
        An' muckle wame,   stomach
In some bit brugh to represent   burgh
        A bailie's name?   magistrate's

Or is't the paughty feudal thane,
Wi' ruffl'd sark an' glancing cane,
Wha thinks himsel nae sheep-shank bane,
                    But lordly stalks,
While caps an' bonnets off are taen,
                    As by he walks?

'O Thou wha gies us each guid gift!
Gie me o' wit an' sense a lift,
Then turn me, if Thou please, adrift
                    Thro' Scotland wide;
Wi' cits nor lairds I wadna shift,
                    In a' their pride!'

Were this the charter of our state,
'On pain o' hell be rich an' great,'
Damnation then would be our fate,
                    Beyond remead;
But, thanks to heaven, that's no the gate
                    We learn our creed.

For thus the royal mandate ran,
When first the human race began:
'The social, friendly, honest man,
                    Whate'er he be,
'Tis he fulfils great Nature's plan,
                    And none but he.'

O mandate glorious and divine!
The followers o' the ragged Nine,
Poor, thoughtless devils! yet may shine
                    In glorious light;
While sordid sons o' Mammon's line
                    Are dark as night!

Tho' here they scrape, an' squeeze, an' growl,
Their worthless nievefu' of a soul
May in some future carcase howl,
                    The forest's fright;
Or in some day-detesting owl
                    May shun the light.

Then may Lapraik and Burns arise,
To reach their native, kindred skies,
And sing their pleasures, hopes an' joys,
                    In some mild sphere;
Still closer knit in friendship's ties,
                    Each passing year!

Margin glosses:
haughty
shirt; shining
load
remedy
way
fistful

Epistle to a Young Friend

May 1786

I lang hae thought, my youthfu' friend,
    A something to have sent you,
Tho' it should serve nae ither end
    Than just a kind memento;
But how the subject-theme may gang,
    Let time and chance determine:
Perhaps it may turn out a sang;
    Perhaps, turn out a sermon.

Ye'll try the world soon, my lad;
    And, Andrew dear, believe me,
Ye'll find mankind an unco squad,   *strange*
    And muckle they may grieve ye:
For care and trouble set your thought,
    Ev'n when your end's attainéd;
And a' your views may come to nought,
    Where ev'ry nerve is strainéd.

I'll no say, men are villains a':
    The real, harden'd wicked,
Wha hae nae check but human law,
    Are to a few restricked;
But, och! mankind are unco weak   *mighty*
    An' little to be trusted;
If Self the wavering balance shake,
    It's rarely right adjusted!

Yet they wha fa' in Fortune's strife,
    Their fate we should na censure;
For still, th' important end of life
    They equally may answer:
A man may hae an honest heart,
    Tho' poortith hourly stare him;   *poverty*
A man may tak a neebor's part,
    Yet hae nae cash to spare him.

Ay free, aff han', your story tell,
    When wi' a bosom cronie;
But still keep something to yoursel
    Ye scarcely tell to onie.
Conceal yoursel as weel's ye can
    Frae critical dissection:
But keek thro' ev'ry other man   *pry*
    'Wi' sharpen'd, sly inspection.

flame
The sacred lowe o' weel-plac'd love,
    Luxuriantly indulge it;
attempt
But never tempt th' illicit rove,
    Tho' naething should divulge it:
I waive the quantum o' the sin,
    The hazard of concealing;
But, och! it hardens a' within,
    And petrifies the feeling!

To catch Dame Fortune's golden smile,
    Assiduous wait upon her;
And gather gear by ev'ry wile
    That's justify'd by honor:
Not for to hide it in a hedge,
    Nor for a train-attendant;
But for the glorious privilege
    Of being independent.

The fear o' Hell's a hangman's whip
    To haud the wretch in order;
But where ye feel your honour grip,
    Let that ay be your border:
Its slightest touches, instant pause—
    Debar a' side-pretences;
And resolutely keep its laws,
    Uncaring consequences.

The great Creator to revere
    Must sure become the creature;
But still the preaching cant forbear,
    And ev'n the rigid feature:
Yet ne'er with wits profane to range
    Be complaisance extended;
An atheist-laugh's a poor exchange
    For Deity offended!

frolicking
When ranting round in Pleasure's ring,
    Religion may be blinded;
Or if she gie a random sting,
    It may be little minded;
But when on Life we're tempest-driv'n—
    A conscience but a canker—
A correspondence fix'd wi' Heav'n
    Is sure a noble anchor!

Adieu, dear, amiable youth!
    Your heart can ne'er be wanting!
May prudence, fortitude, and truth,
    Erect your brow undaunting!
In ploughman phrase 'God send you speed,'
    Still daily to grow wiser;
heed the advice
And may ye better reek the rede
    Than ever did th' Adviser!

To William Creech

Auld chuckie Reekie's* sair distrest,   mother-hen
Down droops her ance weel burnish'd crest,
Nae joy her bonie buskit nest   trimmed
    Can yield ava: at all
Her darling bird that she lo'es best,
    Willie's awa.

O, Willie was a witty wight,
And had o' things an unco sleight!   in; uncommon skill
Auld Reekie ay he keepit tight   in order
    And trig an' braw;   trim; handsome
But now they'll busk her like a fright—   garb
    Willie's awa!

The stiffest o' them a' he bow'd;
The bauldest o' them a' he cow'd;   daunted
They durst nae mair than he allow'd
    That was a law:
We've lost a birkie weel worth gowd— lively fellow; gold
    Willie's awa!

Now gawkies, tawpies, gowks,† and fools
Frae colleges and boarding schools
May sprout like simmer puddock-stools mushrooms
    In glen or shaw: wood
He wha could brush them down to mools, dust
    Willie's awa!

The brethren o' the Commerce-Chaumer
May mourn their loss wi' doolfu' clamour: woful
He was a dictionar and grammar
    Amang them a'.
I fear they'll now mak monie a stammer:
    Willie's awa!

Nae mair we see his levee door
Philosophers and Poets pour,
And toothy Critics by the score
    In bloody raw:
The adjutant of a' the core,
    Willie's awa!

Now worthy Greg'ry's Latin face,
Tytler's and Greenfield's modest grace,
M'Kenzie, Stewart, such a brace
    As Rome ne'er saw,
They a' maun meet some ither place—   must
    Willie's awa!

*Auld Reekie is Edinburgh
†All different words for 'fools'.

	Poor Burns ev'n 'Scotch Drink' canna quicken:
peeps	He cheeps like some bewilder'd chicken
mother; brood	Scar'd frae its minnie and the cleckin
carrion-crow	By hoodie-craw.
	Grief's gien his heart an unco kickin—
	Willie's awa!

ill-tongued, snarling railer   Now ev'ry sour-mou'd, girnin blellum,
kill   And Calvin's folk, are fit to fell him;
Each; scullion   Ilk self-conceited critic-skellum
       His quill may draw:
finely repel assault   He wha could brawlie ward their bellum,
       Willie's awa!

meandering   Up wimpling, stately Tweed I've sped,
   And Eden scenes on crystal Jed,
   And Ettrick banks, now roaring red
       While tempests blaw;
   But every joy and pleasure's fled:
       Willie's awa!

   May I be Slander's common speech,
   A text for Infamy to preach,
stretched   And, lastly, streekit out to bleach
       In winter snaw,
   When I forgot thee, Willie Creech,
       Tho' far awa!

   May never wicked Fortune touzle him,
   May never wicked men bamboozle him,
poll; old as   Until a pow as auld's Methusalem
cheerfully scratch   He canty claw:
   Then to the blessed new Jerusalem
       Fleet-wing awa!

To a Louse

On Seeing One on a Lady's Bonnet at Church

Ha! whare ye gaun, ye crowlan ferlie?
Your impudence protects you sairly:
I canna say but ye strunt rarely
       Owre gauze and lace,
Tho' faith! I fear ye dine but sparely
       On sic a place.

Ye ugly, creepan, blastit wonner,
Detested, shunn'd by saunt an' sinner,
How daur ye set your fit upon her—   foot
        Sae fine a lady!
Gae somewhere else and seek your dinner
        On some poor body.

Swith! in some beggar's hauffet squattle: Off!; temples squat
There ye may creep, and sprawl, and sprattle,   scramble
Wi' ither kindred, jumping cattle,
        In shoals and nations;
Whare horn nor bane ne'er daur unsettle
        Your thick plantations.

Now haud you there! ye're out o' sight,   keep
Below the fatt'rils, snug an' tight;   ribbon ends
Na, faith ye yet! ye'll no be right,
        Till ye've got on it —
The vera tapmost, tow'ring height
        O' Miss's bonnet.

My sooth! right bauld ye set your nose out,
As plump an' grey as onie grozet: gooseberry
O for some rank, mercurial rozet,   rosin
        Or fell, red smeddum,   deadly; powder
I'd gie ye sic a hearty dose o't,
        Wad dress your droddum!   backside

I wad na been surpris'd to spy   would not have
You on an auld wife's flainen toy;   flannel cap
Or aiblins some bit duddie boy,   maybe; small ragged
        On's wyliecoat;   undervest
But Miss's fine Lunardi! fye!   balloon-shaped bonnet
        How daur ye do't?

O Jenny, dinna toss your head,
An' set your beauties a' abroad!   abroad
Ye little ken what cursèd speed
        The blastie's makin!
Thae winks an' finger-ends, I dread,   Those
        Are notice takin!

O wad some Power the giftie gie us
To see oursels as others see us!
It wad frae monie a blunder free us,
        An' foolish notion:
What airs in dress an' gait wad lea'e us,
        An' ev'n devotion!

To a Haggis

jolly	Fair fa' your honest, sonsie face,
	Great chieftain o' the puddin-race!
Above	Aboon them a' ye tak your place,
Paunch; small guts	Painch, tripe, or thairm:
	Weel are ye wordy of a grace
	As lang's my arm.

	The groaning trencher there ye fill,
buttocks	Your hurdies like a distant hill,
skewer	Your pin wad help to mend a mill
	In time o' need,
	While thro' your pores the dews distil
	Like amber bead.

wipe	His knife see rustic Labour dight,
skill	An' cut ye up wi' ready slight,
	Trenching your gushing entrails bright,
	Like onie ditch;
	And then, O what a glorious sight,
	Warm-reekin, rich!

spoon	Then, horn for horn, they stretch an' strive:
	Deil tak the hindmost, on they drive,
bellies; by and by	Till a' their weel-swall'd kytes belyve
	Are bent like drums;
burst	Then auld Guidman, maist like to rive,
	'Bethankit!' hums.

	Is there that owre his French *ragout*,
sicken	Or *olio* that wad staw a sow,
	Or *fricassee* wad mak her spew
disgust	Wi' perfect sconner,
	Looks down wi' sneering, scornfu' view
	On sic a dinner?

	Poor devil! see him owre his trash,
weak; rush	As feckless as a wither'd rash,
	His spindle shank a guid whip-lash,
fist; nut	His nieve a nit;
	Thro' bluidy flood or field to dash,
	O how unfit!

	But mark the Rustic, haggis-fed,
	The trembling earth resounds his tread,
ample	Clap in his walie nieve a blade,
	He'll make it whissle;
crop	An' legs, an' arms, an' heads will sned
	Like taps o' thrissle.

Ye Pow'rs, wha mak mankind your care,
And dish them out their bill o' fare,
Auld Scotland wants nae skinking ware,   watery
                That jaups in luggies: splashes; bowl with
But, if ye wish her gratefu' prayer,   handles
                Gie her a Haggis!

Address to the Deil

O Prince, O Chief of many throned pow'rs,
That led th' embattl'd seraphim to war.

MILTON

O Thou! whatever title suit thee —   Cloven-footed
Auld Hornie, Satan, Nick, or Clootie —
Wha in yon cavern grim an' sootie,
                Clos'd under hatches,
Spairges about the brunstane cootie,   Splashes; dish
                To scaud poor wretches!   scald

Hear me, Auld Hangie, for a wee,   Hangman
An' let poor damned bodies be;
I'm sure sma' pleasure it can gie,
                Ev'n to a deil,
To skelp an' scaud poor dogs like me   spank; scald
                An' hear us squeel.

Great is thy pow'r an' great thy fame;
Far kend an' noted is thy name;
An' tho' yon lowin heugh's thy hame,   flaming hollow
                Thou travels far;
An' faith! thou's neither lag, nor lame,   backward
                Nor blate, nor scaur.   bashful; afraid

Whyles, ranging like a roarin lion,   Now
For prey, a' holes an' corners trying;
Whyles, on the strong-wing'd tempest flyin,
                Tirlan the kirks;   Stripping
Whyles, in the human bosom pryin,
                Unseen thou lurks.

I've heard my rev'rend graunie say,
In lanely glens ye like to stray;
Or, where auld ruin'd castles grey
                Nod to the moon,
Ye fright the nightly wand'rer's way
                Wi' eldritch croon.   ghastly

71

When twilight did my graunie summon,
To say her pray'rs, douce, honest woman,
Aft yont the dyke she's heard you bummin,
   Wi' eerie drone;
Or, rustlin, thro' the boortrees comin,
   Wi' heavy groan.

Ae dreary, windy, winter night,
The stars shot down wi' sklentin light,
Wi' you, mysel, I gat a fright:
   Ayont the lough,
Ye, like a rash-buss, stood in sight;
   Wi' waving sugh.

The cudgel in my nieve did shake,
Each bristl'd hair stood like a stake;
When wi' an eldritch, stoor "quaick, quaick,"
   Amang the springs,
Awa ye squatter'd like a drake,
   On whistling wings.

Let warlocks grim, an' wither'd hags,
Tell how wi' you, on ragweed nags,
They skim the muirs an' dizzy crags,
   Wi' wicked speed;
And in kirk-yards renew their leagues,
   Owre howkit dead.

Thence, countra wives, wi' toil an' pain,
May plunge an' plunge the kirn in vain;
For Och! the yellow treasure's taen
   By witching skill;
An' dawtit, twal-pint hawkie's gaen
   As yell's the bill.

Thence, mystic knots mak great abuse
On young guidmen, fond, keen an' croose;
When the best wark-lume i' the house,
   By cantraip wit,
Is instant made no worth a louse,
   Just at the bit.

When thowes dissolve the snawy hoord,
An' float the jinglin icy boord,
Then water-kelpies haunt the foord,
   By your direction,
An' nighted trav'llers are allur'd
   To their destruction.

Marginal glosses:

- sedate
- beyond
- alders
- One
- squinting
- pond
- clump of rushes
- moan
- fist
- harsh
- ragwort
- exhumed
- churn
- petted, twelve-pint cow
- gone dry as; bull
- husbands;
- merry or cocksure
- tool
- magic
- critical moment
- thaws; hoard

And aft your moss-traversing spunkies   bog; will-o'-the-wisps
Decoy the wight that late an' drunk is:
The bleezin, curst, mischievous monkies
        Delude his eyes,
Till in some miry slough he sunk is,
        Ne'er mair to rise.

When Masons' mystic word an' grip
In storms an' tempests raise you up,
Some cock or cat your rage maun stop,   must
        Or, strange to tell!
The youngest brother ye wad whip
        Aff straught to hell.   straight

Lang syne in Eden's bonie yard,   garden
When youthfu' lovers first were pair'd,
An' all the soul of love they shar'd,
        The raptur'd hour
Sweet on the fragrant flow'ry swaird,
        In shady bow'r:

Then you, ye auld, snick-drawing dog!   crafty
Ye cam to Paradise incog,
An' play'd on man a cursèd brogue   trick
        (Black be you fa'!),
An' gied the infant warld a shog,   shake
        'Maist ruin'd a'.

D'ye mind that day when in a bizz   flurry
Wi' reekit duds, an' reestit gizz,   smoky; scorched wig
Ye did present your smoutie phiz   smutty
        'Mang better folk;
An' sklented on the man of Uzz   squinted
        Your spitefu' joke?

An, how ye gat him i' your thrall,
An' brak him out o' house an' hal',
While scabs an' botches did him gall,   blotches
        Wi' bitter claw;
An' lows'd his ill-tongu'd wicked scaul —   loosed; scold
        Was warst ava?   of all

But a' your doings to rehearse,
Your wily snares an' fechtin fierce,   fighting
Sin' that day Michael did you pierce
        Down to this time,
Wad ding a Lallan tongue, or Erse,   beat; Lowland
        In prose or rhyme.

An' now, Auld Cloots, I ken ye're thinkin,

roistering   A certain Bardie's rantin, drinkin,

hurrying   Some luckless hour will send him linkin,
                To your black Pit;

dodging   But, faith! he'll turn a corner jinkin,
                An' cheat you yet.

But fare-you-weel, Auld Nickie-Ben!

O' wad ye tak a thought an' men'!

perhaps   Ye aiblins might — I dinna ken —
                Still hae a stake:

sad   I'm wae to think upo' yon den,
                Ev'n for your sake!

Descriptive and Narrative Poems

The Cotter's Saturday Night

Inscribed to R. Aiken, Esq.

Let not Ambition mock their useful toil,
Their homely joys, and destiny obscure;
Nor Grandeur hear, with a disdainful smile,
The short and simple annals of the poor.

GRAY

wail   November chill blaws loud wi' angry sugh;
    The short'ning winter-day is near a close;
The miry beasts retreating frae the pleugh;
    The black'ning trains o' craws to their repose:
The toil-worn Cotter frae his labor goes,
    This night his weekly moil is at an end,
Collects his spades, his mattocks, and his hoes,
    Hoping the morn in ease and rest to spend,
And weary, o'er the moor, his course does hameward bend.

74

At length his lonely cot appears in view,
    Beneath the shelter of an aged tree;
Th' expectant wee-things, toddlin, stacher
    through   *totter*
    To meet their dad, wi' flichterin' noise and glee.   *fluttering*
His wee bit ingle, blinkin bonilie,
    His clean hearth-stane, his thrifty wifie's smile,
The lisping infant, prattling on his knee,
    Does a' his weary carking cares beguile,
And makes him quite forget his labor and his toil.

Belyve, the elder bairns come drapping in,   *By and by*
    At service out, amang the farmers roun';
Some ca' the pleugh, some herd, some tentie rin   *follow; heedful run*
    A cannie errand to a neebor toun: *quiet*
Their eldest hope, their Jenny, woman grown,
    In youthfu' bloom, love sparkling in her e'e,
Comes hame, perhaps, to show a braw new gown,
    Or deposite her sair-won penny-fee,   *hard-; wages*
To help her parents dear, if they in hardship be.

With joy unfeign'd, brothers and sisters meet,
    And each for other's weelfare kindly spiers: *asks*
The social hours, swift-wing'd, unnotic'd fleet;
    Each tells the uncos that he sees or hears.   *strange news*
The parents partial eye their hopeful years;
    Anticipation forward points the view;
The mother, wi' her needle and her sheers,
    Gars auld claes look amaist as weel's the new;
The father mixes a' wi' admonition due.   *Makes; clothes*

Their master's and their mistress's command
    The younkers a' are warned to obey;
And mind their labors wi' an eydent hand,   *diligent*
    And ne'er, tho' out o' sight, to jauk or play: *trifle*
'And O! be sure to fear the Lord alway,
    And mind your duty, duly, morn and night;
Lest in temptation's path ye gang astray,
    Implore His counsel and assisting might:
They never sought in vain that sought the Lord aright.'

But hark! a rap comes gently to the door;
    Jenny, wha kens the meaning o' the same,
Tells how a neebor lad came o'er the moor,
    To do some errands, and convoy her hame.
The wily mother sees the conscious flame
    Sparkle in Jenny's e'e, and flush her cheek;
With heart-struck, anxious care, enquires his
    name,
    While Jenny hafflins is afraid to speak;   *half*
Weel-pleas'd the mother hears, it's nae wild, worthless rake.

With kindly welcome, Jenny brings him ben; — *inside*
 A strappin' youth, he takes the mother's eye;
Blythe Jenny sees the visit's no ill taen;
 The father cracks of horses, pleughs, and kye. — *chats; cattle*
The youngster's artless heart o'erflows wi' joy,
 But blate and laithfu', scarce can weel behave; — *shy; sheepish*
The mother, wi' a woman's wiles, can spy
 What makes the youth sae bashfu' and sae
  grave;
Weel-pleas'd to think her bairn's respected like the lave. — *rest*

O happy love! where love like this is found:
 O heart-felt raptures! bliss beyond compare!
I've pacèd much this weary, mortal round,
 And sage experience bids me this declare:
'If Heaven a draught of heavenly pleasure spare,
 One cordial in this melancholy vale,
'Tis when a youthful, loving, modest pair,
 In other's arms, breathe out the tender tale
Beneath the milk-white thorn that scents that ev'ning gale.'

Is there, in human form, that bears a heart,
 A wretch! a villain! lost to love and truth!
That can, with studied, sly, ensnaring art,
 Betray sweet Jenny's unsuspecting youth?
Curse on his perjur'd arts! dissembling, smooth!
 Are honor, virtue, conscience, all exil'd?
Is there no pity, no relenting ruth,
 Points to the parents fondling o'er their child?
Then paints the ruin'd maid, and their distraction wild?

But now the supper crowns their simple board,
 The healsome porritch, chief o' Scotia's food: — *wholesome*
The soupe their only hawkie does afford, — *milk; cow*
 That 'yont the hallan snugly chows her cood; — *beyond; partition*
The dame brings forth, in complimental mood,
 To grace the lad, her weel-hain'd kebbuck, fell; — *-saved; cheese; pungent*
And aft he's prest, and aft he ca's it guid;
 The frugal wifie, garrulous, will tell,
How 'twas a towmond auld, sin' lint was i' the bell. — *twelve-month; flax; flower*

The chearfu' supper done, wi' serious face,
 They, round the ingle, form a circle wide;
The sire turns o'er, wi' patriarchal grace,
 The big ha'-Bible, ance his father's pride.
His bonnet rev'rently is laid aside,
 His lyart haffets wearing thin and bare; — *grey side-locks*
Those strains that once did sweet in Zion glide,
 He wales a portion with judicious care, — *selects*
'And let us worship God!' he says, with solemn air.

They chant their artless notes in simple guise;
    They tune their hearts, by far the noblest aim:
Perhaps *Dundee's* wild-warbling measures rise,
    Or plaintive *Martyrs*, worthy of the name;
Or noble *Elgin* beets the heaven-ward flame,   fans
    The sweetest far of Scotia's holy lays:
Compar'd with these, Italian trills are tame;
    The tickl'd ears no heart-felt raptures raise;
Nae unison hae they, with our Creator's praise.

The priest-like father reads the sacred page,
    How Abram was the friend of God on high;
Or, Moses bade eternal warfare wage
    With Amalek's ungracious progeny;
Or, how the royal Bard did groaning lie
    Beneath the stroke of Heaven's avenging ire;
Or Job's pathetic plaint, and wailing cry;
    Or rapt Isaiah's wild, seraphic fire;
Or other holy Seers that tune the sacred lyre.

Perhaps the Christian volume is the theme:
    How guiltless blood for guilty man was shed;
How He, who bore in Heaven the second name,
    Had not on earth whereon to lay His head;
How His first followers and servants sped;
    The precepts sage they wrote to many a land:
How he, who lone in Patmos banishèd,
    Saw in the sun a mighty angel stand,
And heard great Bab'lon's doom pronounc'd by
    Heaven's command.

Then kneeling down to Heaven's Eternal King,
    The saint, the father, and the husband prays;
Hope 'springs exulting on triumphant wing,'*
    That thus they all shall meet in future days,
There, ever bask in uncreated rays,
    No more to sigh or shed the bitter tear,
Together hymning their Creator's praise,
    In such society, yet still more dear;
While circling Time moves round in an eternal sphere.

Compar'd with this, how poor Religion's pride,
    In all the pomp of method, and of art,
When men display to congregations wide
    Devotion's ev'ry grace, except the heart!
The Power, incens'd, the pageant will desert,
    The pompous strain, the sacerdotal stole;
But haply, in some cottage far apart,
    May hear, well-pleas'd, the language of the
    soul,
And in His Book of Life the inmates poor enroll.

* Pope's *Windsor Forest*. (Burns's note.)

Then homeward all take off their sev'ral way;
    The youngling cottagers retire to rest:
The parent-pair their secret homage pay,
    And proffer up to Heaven the warm request,
That He who stills the raven's clam'rous nest,
    And decks the lily fair in flow'ry pride,
Would, in the way His wisdom sees the best,
    For them and for their little ones provide;
But, chiefly, in their hearts with Grace divine
    preside.

From scenes like these, old Scotia's grandeur
    springs,
    That makes her lov'd at home, rever'd abroad:
Princes and lords are but the breath of kings,
    'An honest man's the noblest work of God';
And certes, in fair Virtue's heavenly road,
    The cottage leaves the palace far behind:
What is a lordling's pomp? a cumbrous load,
    Disguising oft the wretch of human kind,
Studied in arts of Hell, in wickedness refin'd!

O Scotia! my dear, my native soil!
    For whom my warmest wish to Heaven is sent!
Long may thy hardy sons of rustic toil
    Be blest with health and peace and sweet
    content!
And O! may Heaven their simple lives prevent
    From Luxury's contagion, weak and vile!
Then, how'er crowns and coronets be rent,
    A virtuous populace may rise the while,
And stand a wall of fire around their much-lov'd Isle.

O Thou! who pour'd the patriotic tide,
    That stream'd thro' great, unhappy Wallace'
    heart,
Who dar'd to, nobly, stem tyrannic pride,
    Or nobly die, the second glorious part:
(The patriot's God, peculiarly Thou art,
    His friend, inspirer, guardian, and reward!)
O never, never Scotia's realm desert;
    But still the patriot, and the patriot-bard
In bright succession raise, her ornament and guard!

Tam o' Shanter

A Tale

Of Brownyis and of Bogillis full in this buke.
GAWIN DOUGLAS

When chapman billies leave the street, — pedlar fellows
And drouthy neebors neebors meet; — thirsty
As market-days are wearing late,
An' folk begin to tak the gate; — road
While we sit bousing at the nappy, — ale
An' getting fou and unco happy, — drunk; mighty
We think na on the lang Scots miles, — not
The mosses, waters, slaps, and styles, — bogs; pools; breaches; stiles
That lie between us and our hame,
Whare sits our sulky, sullen dame,
Gathering her brows like gathering storm,
Nursing her wrath to keep it warm.

This truth fand honest Tam o' Shanter, — found
As he frae Ayr ae night did canter: — one
(Auld Ayr, wham ne'er a town surpasses,
For honest men and bonie lasses.)

O Tam, had'st thou but been sae wise,
As taen thy ain wife Kate's advice! — to have taken
She tauld thee weel thou was a skellum, — good-for-nothing
A blethering, blustering, drunken blellum; — chattering; babbler
That frae November till October,
Ae market-day thou was nae sober;
That ilka melder wi' the miller, — every meal-grinding
Thou sat as lang as thou had siller; — money
That ev'ry naig was ca'd a shoe on, — called
The smith and thee gat roaring fou on;
That at the Lord's house, even on Sunday,
Thou drank wi' Kirkton Jean till Monday.
She prophesied, that, late or soon,
Thou would be found deep drown'd in Doon,
Or catch'd wi' warlocks in the mirk — dark
By Alloway's auld, haunted kirk.

Ah! gentle dames, it gars me greet, — makes; weep
To think how monie counsels sweet,
How monie lengthen'd, sage advices
The husband frae the wife despises!

	But to our tale: Ae market-night,
uncommonly	Tam had got planted unco right,
	Fast by an ingle, bleezing finely,
foaming new ale	Wi' reaming swats, that drank divinely;
Cobbler	And at his elbow, Souter Johnie,
thirsty	His ancient, trusty, drouthy cronie:

But to our tale: Ae market-night,
Tam had got planted unco right,
Fast by an ingle, bleezing finely,
Wi' reaming swats, that drank divinely;
And at his elbow, Souter Johnie,
His ancient, trusty, drouthy cronie:
Tam lo'ed him like a very brither;
They had been fou for weeks thegither.
The night drave on wi' sangs and clatter;
And ay the ale was growing better:
The landlady and Tam grew gracious
Wi' secret favours, sweet and precious:
The Souter tauld his queerest stories;
The landlord's laugh was ready chorus:
roar The storm without might rair and rustle,
Tam did na mind the storm a whistle.

ale Care, mad to see a man sae happy,
E'en drown'd himsel amang the nappy.
As bees flee hame wi' lades o' treasure,
The minutes wing'd their way wi' pleasure:
Kings may be blest but Tam was glorious,
O'er a' the ills o' life victorious!

But pleasures are like poppies spread:
You seize the flow'r, its bloom is shed;
Or like the snow falls in the river,
A moment white — then melts for ever;
Or like the Borealis race,
That flit ere you can point their place;
Or like the rainbow's lovely form
Evanishing amid the storm.
Nae man can tether time or tide;
must The hour approaches Tam maun ride:
That hour, o' night's black arch the key-stane,
That dreary hour Tam mounts his beast in;
And sic a night he taks the road in,
As ne'er poor sinner was abroad in.

would have The wind blew as 'twad blawn its last;
The rattling showers rose on the blast;
The speedy gleams the darkness swallow'd;
Loud, deep, and lang the thunder bellow'd:
That night, a child might understand,
The Deil had business on his hand.

Weel mounted on his gray mare Meg,
A better never lifted leg,
Tam skelpit on thro' dub and mire,   *spanked; puddle*
Despising wind, and rain, and fire;
Whiles holding fast his guid blue bonnet,   *Now*
Whiles crooning o'er some auld Scots sonnet,   *song*
Whiles glow'ring round wi' prudent cares,   *staring*
Lest bogles catch him unawares: *ghosts*
Kirk-Alloway was drawing nigh,
Whare ghaists and houlets nightly cry.   *owls*

By this time he was cross the ford,   *across*
Whare in the snaw the chapman smoor'd;   *smothered*
And past the birks and meikle stane,   *birches; big*
Whare drunken Charlie brak's neck-bane;
And thro' the whins, and by the cairn,   *furze; pile of stones*
Whare hunters fand the murder'd bairn;
And near the thorn, aboon the well,   *above*
Where Mungo's mither hang'd hersel.
Before him Doon pours all his floods;
The doubling storm roars thro' the woods;
The lightnings flash from pole to pole;
Near and more near the thunders roll:
When, glimmering thro' the groaning trees,
Kirk-Alloway seemed in a bleeze,
Thro' ilka bore the beams were glancing,   *chink*
And loud resounded mirth and dancing.

Inspiring, bold John Barleycorn!
What dangers thou canst make us scorn!
Wi' tippenny, we fear nae evil: *ale*
Wi' usquabae, we'll face the Devil!   *whisky*
The swats sae ream'd in Tammie's noddle,
Fair play, he car'd na deils a boddle.   *not; farthing*
But Maggie stood, right sair astonish'd,
Till, by the heel and hand admonish'd,
She ventur'd forward on the light;
And, wow! Tam saw an unco sight!   *wondrous*

Warlocks and witches in a dance:
Nae cotillion, brent new frae France,   *brand*
But hornpipes, jigs, strathspeys, and reels,
Put life and mettle in their heels.
A winnock-bunker in the east,   *window-seat*
There sat Auld Nick, in shape o' beast;
A tousie tyke, black, grim, and large,   *shaggy dog*
To gie them music was his charge:
He screw'd the pipes and gart them skirl,   *shriek*
Till roof and rafters a' did dirl.   *ring*
Coffins stood round, like open presses,   *cupboards*
That shaw'd the dead in their last dresses;
And, by some devilish cantraip sleight,   *magic device*

Each in its cauld hand held a light:
By which heroic Tam was able
To note upon the haly table,
-irons A murderer's banes, in gibbet-airns;
Twa span-lang, wee, unchristen'd bairns;
A thief new-cutted frae a rape —
mouth Wi' his last gasp his gab did gape;
Five tomahawks wi' bluid red-rusted;
Five scymitars wi' murder crusted:
A garter which a babe had strangled;
A knife a father's throat had mangled —
Whom his ain son o' life bereft —
The grey hairs yet stack to the heft:
Wi' mair of horrible and awefu',
Which even to name wad be unlawfu'.

stared   As Tammie glowr'd, amaz'd, and curious,
The mirth and fun grew fast and furious;
The piper loud and louder blew,
The dancers quick and quicker flew,
each old woman They reel'd, they set, they cross'd, they cleekit,
sweated and steamed Till ilka carlin swat and reekit,
rags And coost her duddies to the wark,
tripped; shift And linket at it in her sark!

these; young girls   Now Tam, O Tam, had thae been queans,
A' plump and strapping in their teens!
greasy Their sarks, instead o' creeshie flannen,
Been snaw-white seventeen hunder linen!*

These Thir breeks o' mine, my only pair,
That ance were plush, o' guid blue hair,
buttocks I wad hae gi'en them off my hurdies
girls For ae blink o' the bonie burdies!

Withered; wean   But wither'd beldams, auld and droll,
Rigwoodie hags wad spean a foal,
leaping; kicking; cudgel Louping and flinging on a crummock,
I wonder didna turn thy stomach!

well   But Tam kend what was what fu' brawlie:
comely; choice There was ae winsome wench and wawlie,
company That night enlisted in the core,
Lang after kend on Carrick shore
death (For monie a beast to dead she shot,
An' perish'd monie a bonie boat,
much; barley And shook baith meikle corn and bear,
And kept the country-side in fear.)
short shift; coarse cloth Her cutty sark, o' Paisley harn,
That while a lassie she had worn,
In longitude tho' sorely scanty,

* Linen woven with 1,700 threads to the warp.

82

It was her best, and she was vauntie.   proud
Ah! little kend thy reverend grannie,
That sark she coft for her wee Nannie,   bought
Wi' twa pund Scots ('twas a' her riches,)
Wad ever grac'd a dance of witches!   Would have

But here my Muse her wing maun cour,   lower
Sic flights as far beyond her power:
To sing how Nannie lap and flang   leaped and kicked
(A souple jad she was and strang;)
And how Tam stood like ane bewitch'd,
And thought his very een enrich'd;   eyes
Even Satan glowr'd, and fidg'd fu' fain,   twitched with excitement
And hotch'd and blew wi' might and main;   jerked
Till first ae caper, syne anither,   then
Tam tint his reason a' thegither,   lost
And roars out: 'Weel done, Cutty-sark!'
And in an instant all was dark;
And scarcely had he Maggie rallied,
When out the hellish legion sallied.

As bees bizz out wi' angry fyke,   fret
When plundering herds assail their byke;   hive
As open pussie's mortal foes,   the hare's
When, pop! she starts before their nose;
As eager runs the market-crowd,
When 'Catch the thief!' resounds aloud:
So Maggie runs, the witches follow,
Wi' mony an eldritch skreech and hollow.   unearthly

Ah, Tam! Ah, Tam! thou'll get thy fairin!
In hell they'll roast thee like a herrin!
In vain thy Kate awaits thy comin!
Kate soon will be a woefu' woman!
Now, do thy speedy utmost, Meg,
And win the key-stane of the brig;
There, at them thou thy tail may toss,
A running stream they dare na cross!
But ere the key-stane she could make,
The fient a tail she had to shake: devil
For Nannie, far before the rest,
Hard upon noble Maggie's prest,
And flew at Tam wi' furious ettle;   aim
But little wist she Maggie's mettle!
Ae spring brought off her master hale,   whole
But left behind her ain grey tail:
The carlin claught her by the rump,   seized
And left poor Maggie scarce a stump.

Now, wha this tale o' truth shall read,
Ilk man, and mother's son, take heed:
Whene'er to drink you are inclin'd,
Or cutty sarks run in your mind,
Think! ye may buy the joys o'er dear:
Remember Tam o' Shanter's mare.

Songs

Mary Morison

O Mary, at thy window be!
   It is the wish'd, the trysted hour.
Those smiles and glances let me see,
   That make the miser's treasure poor.
   How blythely wad I bide the stoure, *bear the struggle*
A weary slave frae sun to sun,
   Could I the rich reward secure,
The lovely Mary Morison!

Yestreen when to the trembling string *Last night*
   The dance gaed thro' the lighted ha', *went*
To thee my fancy took its wing,
   I sat, but neither heard nor saw:
   Tho' this was fair, and that was braw, *fine*
And yon the toast of a' the town, *the other*
   I sigh'd and said amang them a',
'Ye are na Mary Morison!'

O Mary, canst thou wreck his peace
   Wha for thy sake wad gladly die?
Or canst thou break that heart of his
   Whase only faut is loving thee? *fault*
   If love for love thou wilt na gie, *give*
At least be pity to me shown:
   A thought ungentle canna be *cannot*
The thought o' Mary Morison.

84

There Was a Lad

Robin was a rovin boy,
,Rantin, rovin, rantin, rovin,   roistering
Robin was a rovin boy,
Rantin, rovin Robin.

There was a lad was born in Kyle,
But whatna day o' whatna style,*   what
I doubt it's hardly worth the while
   To be sae nice wi' Robin.   particular
     Robin was &c.

Our monarch's hindmost year but ane   one
Was five-and-twenty days begun,
'Twas then a blast o' Janwar' win'   January wind
   Blew hansel in on Robin.   new-year gift
     Robin was &c.

The gossip keekit in his loof,   glanced; palm
Quo' scho: 'Wha lives will see the proof,   Quoth she
This waly boy will be nae coof: thumping; dolt
   I think we'll ca' him Robin.
     Robin was &c.

'He'll hae misfortunes great an' sma',
But ay a heart aboon them a'.   above
He'll be a credit till us a':   to
   We'll a' be proud o' Robin!
     Robin was &c.

'But sure as three times three mak nine,
I see by ilka score and line,   every
This chap will dearly like our kin',   kind
   So leeze me on thee, Robin!   my blessings
     Robin was &c.

'Guid faith,' quo' scho, 'I doubt you gar   make
The bonie lasses lie aspar;   aspread
But twenty fauts ye may hae waur —   faults; worse
   So blessins on thee, Robin!'
     Robin was &c.

* 'on what day and by what method of dating'. (The reformed calendar was adopted in Britain in 1751.)

Up in the Morning Early

Cauld blaws the wind frae east to west,
　　The drift is driving sairly;
shrill　Sae loud and shill's I hear the blast,
　　I'm sure it's winter fairly.
Up in the morning's no for me,
　　Up in the morning early;
When a' the hills are cover'd wi' snaw,
　　I'm sure it's winter fairly.

The birds sit chattering in the thorn,
　　A' day they fare but sparely;
And lang's the night frae e'en to morn,
　　I'm sure it's winter fairly.
Up in the morning's no for me,
　　Up in the morning early;
When a' the hills are cover'd wi' snaw,
　　I'm sure it's winter fairly.

I Love my Jean

directions　Of a' the airts the wind can blaw
　　I dearly like the west,
For there the bony lassie lives,
　　The lassie I lo'e best.
roll　There wild woods grow, and rivers row,
　　And mony a hill between,
But day and night my fancy's flight
　　Is ever wi' my Jean.

I see her in the dewy flowers,
　　I see her sweet and fair.
I hear her in the tunefu' birds,
　　I hear her charm the air.
There's not a bony flower that springs
wood　　By fountain, shaw, or green,
There's not a bony bird that sings,
reminds　　But minds me o' my Jean.

My Bonie Mary

Go, fetch to me a pint o' wine,
　　And fill it in a silver tassie,
That I may drink before I go
　　A service to my bonie lassie!
The boat rocks at the pier o' Leith,
　　Fu' loud the wind blaws frae the Ferry,
The ship rides by the Berwick-Law,
must　　And I maun leave my bonie Mary.

86

The trumpets sound, the banners fly,
   The glittering spears are rankèd ready,
The shouts o' war are heard afar,
   The battle closes deep and bloody.
It's not the roar o' sea or shore
   Wad mak me langer wish to tarry,
Nor shouts o' war that's heard afar:
   It's leaving thee, my bonie Mary!

Afton Water

Flow gently, sweet Afton, among thy green braes,   slopes
Flow gently, I'll sing thee a song in thy praise;
My Mary's asleep by thy murmuring stream,
Flow gently, sweet Afton, disturb not her dream!

Thou stock dove whose echo resounds thro' the
   glen,
Ye wild whistling blackbirds in yon thorny den,
Thou green-crested lapwing, thy screaming forbear—
I charge you, disturb not my slumbering Fair.

How lofty, sweet Afton, thy neighbouring hills,
Far mark'd with the courses of clear, winding rills;
There daily I wander, as noon rises high,
My flocks and my Mary's sweet cot in my eye.

How pleasant thy banks and green vallies below,
Where wild in the woodlands the primroses blow;
There oft, as mild ev'ning weeps over the lea,
The sweet-scented birk shades my Mary and me.   birch

Thy crystal stream, Afton, how lovely it glides,
And winds by the cot where my Mary resides;
How wanton thy waters her snowy feet lave,
As, gathering sweet flowerets, she stems thy clear
   wave.

Flow gently, sweet Afton, among thy green braes,
Flow gently, sweet river, the theme of my lays;
My Mary's asleep by thy murmuring stream,
Flow gently, sweet Afton, disturb not her dream.

Ay Waukin, O

CHORUS
Ay waukin, O,
awake *Waukin still and weary:*
Sleep I can get nane
For thinking of my dearie.

Simmer's a pleasant time:
 Flowers of every colour,
crag The water rins owre the heugh,
 And I long for my true lover.
Ay waukin, &c.

When I sleep I dream,
apprehensive When I wauk I'm eerie,
Sleep I can get nane
 For thinking on my dearie.
Ay waukin, &c.

Lanely night comes on,
rest A' the lave are sleepin:
I think on my bonie lad,
eyes; weeping And I bleer my een wi' greetin.
Ay waukin, &c.

John Anderson My Jo

John Anderson my jo, John,
acquainted When we were first acquent,
Your locks were like the raven,
smooth Your bonie brow was brent;
bald But now your brow is beld, John,
Your locks are like the snaw,
pate But blessings on your frosty pow,
 John Anderson my jo.

John Anderson my jo, John,
climbed; together We clamb the hill thegither,
jolly And monie a cantie day, John,
We've had wi' ane anither:
must Now we maun totter down, John,
 And hand in hand we'll go,
And sleep thegither at the foot,
 John Anderson my jo.

The Banks O' Doon

Ye banks and braes o' bonie Doon,   slopes
  How can ye bloom sae fresh and fair?
How can ye chant, ye little birds,
  And I sae weary fu' o' care!
Thou'll break my heart, thou warbling bird,
  That wantons thro' the flowering thorn:
Thou minds me o' departed joys,
  Departed never to return.

Aft hae I rov'd by bonie Doon
  To see the rose and woodbine twine,
And ilka bird sang o' its luve,   every
  And fondly sae did I o' mine.
Wi' lightsome heart I pu'd a rose,   plucked
  Fu' sweet upon its thorny tree;
And my fause luver staw my rose,   stole
  But ah! he left the thorn wi' me.

Hey, Ca' Thro'

CHORUS

Hey, ca' thro', ca' thro',   work away
For we hae mickle ado,   much to do
Hey, ca' thro', ca' thro',
For we have mickle ado.

Up wi' the carls of Dysart   old men
  And the lads o' Buckhaven,
And the kimmers o' Largo   gossips
  And the lasses o' Leven!
          Hey, ca' thro', &c

We hae tales to tell,
  And we hae sangs to sing;
We hae pennies to spend,
  And we hae pints to bring.
          Hey, ca' thro', &c.

We'll live a' our days,
  And them that comes behin',
Let them do the like,
  And spend the gear they win!   wealth
          Hey, ca' thro', &c.

The Deil's Awa wi' th' Exciseman

The Deil's awa, the Deil's awa,
The Deil's awa wi' th' Exciseman!
He's danc'd awa, he's danc'd awa,
He's danc'd awa wi' th' Exciseman!

The Deil cam fiddlin thro' the town,
  And danc'd awa wi' th' Exciseman,
every; And ilka wife cries 'Auld Mahoun,
  I wish you luck o' the prize, man!'
    The Deil's awa, &c.

malt We'll mak our maut, and we'll brew our drink,
  We'll laugh, sing, and rejoice, man,
handsome; big And monie braw thanks to the meikle black Deil,
  That danc'd awa wi' th' Exciseman.
    The Deil's awa, &c.

There's threesome reels, there's foursome reels,
  There's hornpipes and strathspeys, man,
But the ae best dance e'er came to the land
  Was, the Deil's awa wi' th' Exciseman.
    The Deil's awa, &c.

The Lea-Rig

ridge of unploughed grass between arable ridges

When o'er the hill the eastern star
  folding Tells bughtin time is near, my jo,
And owsen frae the furrow'd field
  dull Return sae dowf and weary, O,
Down by the burn, where scented birks
  Wi' dew are hangin clear, my jo,
I'll meet thee on the lea-rig,
  My ain kind dearie, O.

At midnight hour in mirkest glen,
  frightened I'd rove and ne'er be eerie, O,
went If thro' that glen I gaed to thee,
  My ain kind dearie, O.
Altho' the night were ne'er sae wild,
  And I were ne'er sae weary, O,
I'll meet thee on the lea-rig,
  My ain kind dearie, O.

The hunter lo'es the morning sun
   To rouse the mountain deer, my jo;
At noon the fisher takes the glen
   Adown the burn to steer, my jo:
Gie me the hour o' gloamin grey—   twilight
   It maks my heart sae cheery, O,
To meet thee on the lea-rig,
   My ain kind dearie, O.

Duncan Gray

Duncan Gray came here to woo,
   Ha, ha, the wooing o't,
On blythe Yule-Night when we were fou,   Christmas Eve; drunk
   Ha, ha, the wooing o't.
Maggie coost her head fu' high,   cast
Look'd asklent and unco skeigh,   askance; very skittish
Gart poor Duncan stand abeigh;   Made; off
   Ha, ha, the wooing o't.

Duncan fleech'd, and Duncan pray'd;   wheedled
   Ha, ha, the wooing o't,
Meg was deaf as Ailsa Craig,
   Ha, ha, the wooing o't.
Duncan sigh'd baith out and in,   both
Grat his een baith bleer't an' blin',   Wept; eyes
Spak o' lowpin o'er a linn;   leaping; waterfall
   Ha, ha, the wooing o't.

Time and Chance are but a tide,
   Ha, ha, the wooing o't,
Slighted love is sair to bide   hard to endure
   Ha, ha, the wooing o't.
'Shall I like a fool,' quoth he,
'For a haughty hizzie die?   jade
'She may gae to – France for me!'   go
   Ha, ha, the wooing o't.

How it comes let doctors tell,
   Ha, ha, the wooing o't,
Meg grew sick, as he grew hale,
   Ha, ha, the wooing o't.
Something in her bosom wrings,
For relief a sigh she brings,
And O! her een they spak sic things!   such
   Ha, ha, the wooing o't.

Duncan was a lad o' grace,
    Ha, ha, the wooing o't,
Maggie's was a piteous case,
    Ha, ha, the wooing o't.
Duncan could na be her death,
smothered   Swelling pity smoor'd his wrath;
proud; jolly   Now they're crouse and canty baith,
    Ha, ha, the wooing o't.

Robert Bruce's March to Bannockburn

Scots, wha hae wi' Wallace bled,
Scots, wham Bruce has aften led,
Welcome to your gory bed
        Or to victorie!

Now's the day, and now's the hour;
See the front o' battle lour,
See approach proud Edward's power,
        Chains and slaverie.

Wha will be a traitor knave?
Wha can fill a coward's grave?
Wha sae base as be a slave?
        Let him turn and flee.

Wha for Scotland's king and law,
Freedom's sword will strongly draw,
Free-man stand or Free-man fa',
        Let him follow me.

By oppressions woes and pains,
By your sons in servile chains,
We will drain our dearest veins,
        But they *shall* be free!

Lay the proud usurpers low!
Tyrants fall in every foe!
Liberty's in every blow!
        Let us Do or Die!

O, Whistle an' I'll Come to Ye, My Lad

CHORUS

O, whistle an' I'll come to ye, my lad,
O, whistle an' I'll come to ye, my lad,
Tho' father an' mother an' a' should gae mad,   go
O, whistle an' I'll come to ye, my lad.

But warily tent when ye come to court me,   watch
And come nae unless the back-yett be a-jee;   not; -gate; ajar
Syne up the back-style, and let naebody see,   Then
And come as ye were na comin to me,   not
And come as ye were na comin to me.
                    O, whistle &c.

At kirk, or at market, whene'er ye meet me,
Gang by me as tho' that ye car'd na a flie;   Go; fly
But steal me a blink o' your bonie black e'e,   glance
Yet look as ye were na lookin at me,
Yet look as ye were na lookin at me.
                    O, whistle &c.

Ay vow and protest that ye care na for me,
And whyles ye may lightly my beauty a wee;   sometimes; disparage;
But court na anither, tho' jokin ye be,   little
For fear that she wyle your fancy frae me,
For fear that she wyle your fancy frae me.   entice
                    O, whistle &c.

A Red, Red Rose

O my luve's like a red, red rose,
   That's newly sprung in June;
O my luve's like the melodie
   That's sweetly play'd in tune.

As fair art thou, my bonie lass,
   So deep in luve am I,
And I will luve thee still, my Dear,
   Till a' the seas gang dry.   go

Till a' the seas gang dry, my Dear,
   And the rocks melt wi' the sun:
I will luve thee still, my Dear,
   While the sands o' life shall run.

And fare thee weel, my only Luve,
   And fare thee weel a while!
And I will come again, my Luve,
   Tho' it were ten thousand mile!

Ca' the Yowes to the Knowes

Drive; ewes; knolls

brooklet runs

Ca' the yowes to the knowes,
Ca' them where the heather grows,
Ca' them where the burnie rowes,
   My bonie dearie.

thrush's

go

Hark, the mavis' e'ening sang
Sounding Clouden's woods amang,
Then a-faulding let us gang,
   My bonie dearie.
                              Ca' the yowes &c.

We'll gae down by Clouden side,
Through the hazels, spreading wide
O'er the waves that sweetly glide
   To the moon sae clearly.
                              Ca' the yowes &c.

Yonder Clouden's silent towers,
Where, at moonshine's midnight hours,
O'er the dewy bending flowers
   Fairies dance sae cheery.
                              Ca' the yowes &c.

hobgoblin

Ghaist nor bogle shalt thou fear;
Thou'rt to Love and Heav'n sae dear
Nocht of ill may come thee near,
   My bonie dearie.
                              Ca' the yowes &c.

Fair and lovely as thou art,
Thou has stown my very heart;
I can die—but canna part,
   My bonie dearie.
                              Ca' the yowes &c.

For a' That and a' That

Is there for honest poverty
    That hings his head, an' a' that?   hangs
The coward slave, we pass him by,
    We dare be poor for a' that!
For a' that, an' a' that,
    Our toils obscure, an' a' that,
The rank is but the guinea's stamp,
    The man's the gowd for a that.   gold

What though on hamely fare we dine,
    Wear hoddin grey, an' a' that?   coarse grey woollen
Gie fools their silks, and knaves their wine,   cloth
    A man's a man for a' that.
For a' that, an' a' that,
    Their tinsel show, an' a' that,
The honest man, tho' e'er sae poor,
    Is king o' men for a' that.

Ye see yon birkie ca'd a lord,   fellow; called
    Wha struts, an' stares, an' a' that?
Tho' hundreds worship at his word,
    He's but a cuif for a' that.   dolt
For a' that, an' a' that,
    His ribband, star, an' a' that,
The man o' independent mind,
    He looks an' laughs at a' that.

A prince can mak a belted knight,
    A marquis, duke, an' a' that!
But an honest man's aboon his might—   above
    Guid faith, he mauna fa' that!   must not lay claim to
For a' that, an' a' that,
    Their dignities an' a' that,
The pith o' sense an' pride o' worth
    Are higher rank than a' that.

Then let us pray that come it may
    As come it will for a' that,
That Sense and Worth o'er a' the earth
    Shall bear the gree an' a' that.   win; first place
For a' that, an' a' that,
    It's comin yet for a' that,
That man to man the world o'er
    Shall brother be for a' that.

O, Wert Thou in The Cauld Blast

O, wert thou in the cauld blast
   On yonder lea, on yonder lea,
quarter   My plaidie to the angry airt,
   I'd shelter thee, I'd shelter thee.
Or did misfortune's bitter storms
   Around thee blaw, around thee blaw,
shelter   Thy bield should be my bosom,
   To share it a', to share it a'.

Or were I in the wildest waste,
   Sae black and bare, sae black and bare,
The desert were a paradise,
   If thou wert there, if thou wert there.
Or were I monarch o' the globe,
   Wi' thee to reign, wi' thee to reign,
The brightest jewel in my crown
   Wad be my queen, wad be my queen.

Auld Lang Syne

CHORUS

old long ago   *For auld lang syne, my dear,*
   For auld lang syne,
We'll tak a cup o' kindness yet,
   For auld lang syne.

Should auld acquaintance be forgot,
   And never brought to mind?
Should auld acquaintance be forgot,
   And auld lang syne?
   For auld &c.

pay for   And surely ye'll be your pint-stowp!
   And surely I'll be mine!
And we'll tak a cup o' kindness yet,
   For auld lang syne.
   For auld &c.

hill-sides   We twa hae run about the braes
pulled; wild daisies   And pu'd the gowans fine;
But we've wander'd mony a weary foot
since   Sin auld lang syne.
   For auld &c.

waded; brook   We twa hae paidl'd i' the burn
noon   Frae mornin' sun till dine;
broad   But seas between us braid hae roar'd
   Sin auld lang syne.
   For auld &c.

comrade   And there's a hand, my trusty fiere!
give me   And gie's a hand o' thine!
good-will drink   And we'll tak a right gude-willy waught,
   For auld lang syne.
   For auld &c.